Gary McIntosh's book *One Size Doesn't Fit All* is the easiest and most informative book on church leadership I have ever read. Why didn't a few seminary professors teach me this stuff twenty-five years ago? This book will be a classic in the area of church leadership and growth.

Dr. Michael Bradaric, senior pastor,
Magnolia Baptist Church, Anaheim, California

After serving in small, medium, and large churches, I wish this material had been available twenty-five years ago. I wish every church leader would read and apply these principles.

Dr. J. Michael Broyles, executive pastor,
Grace Baptist Church, Santa Clarita, California

Gary McIntosh uses his warm conversational style and vast years of experience in church analysis and consulting to provide a book of wisdom for pastors.

Dr. David H. McKinley, senior pastor,
Boca Raton Community Church, Boca Raton, Florida

One Size Doesn't Fit All is must reading for all church planters or leaders in any size church, especially small ones. As a church planter, my core group will definitely be required to read this book, as will future leaders.

Dr. Hozell C. Francis, church planter,
Southern California

One Size Doesn't Fit All is by far the best book I have read concerning what it takes to grow a church from small to medium to large. This book was extremely enlightening. I feel it is a pinnacle of work that has long been needed.

Dr. Lorenzo V. Gonzalez, church growth and leadership consultant,
Southern California

Today's pastors need "the straight goods" about how churches grow from stage to stage. *One Size Doesn't Fit All* is the road map to get them to the right destination, especially when the way looks uncertain, the personal cost is high, and the obstacles look insurmountable. I found the analysis of each size church to be right on target.

Dr. Jerry Rueb, senior pastor,
South Delta Baptist Church, Delta, BC, Canada

Having ministered in small to mega-churches, I found myself relating to and agreeing with virtually everything that was written. This is a work I will be consulting often for many years to come.

Dr. Ted Martinez, pastor,
Evangelical Free Church, Walnut, California

An essential and concise manual for pastors in any church.

Dr. Mahlon Friesen, senior pastor,
First Baptist Church, Yucaipa, California

This is absolutely a great book. Every denominational leader should make sure that their pastors have a copy of this book. It is the most enjoyable, practical, and capsulated version of church growth dynamics I have ever seen.

Dr. Gil Stieglitz, senior pastor,
Twin Lakes Community Church, Palmdale, California

I wish I would have had this book when I started out as a church planting pastor in 1979. It also would have been helpful for our church at every transition point in its growth journey from a small church to a large-sized church.

Dr. Raleigh Galgan, senior pastor,
Valley Evangelical Free Church, Vacaville, California

If only I had been able to read this book eighteen years ago when I became a pastor. What a difference it would have made! This is the most significant book I have read in the last twenty-four months.

Dr. Mark Belokonny, church consultant,
Vancouver, Washington

Mike Grondelski

One Size
Doesn't Fit All

Bringing Out the Best
in Any Size Church

Gary L. McIntosh

Fleming H. Revell
A Division of Baker Book House Co
Grand Rapids, Michigan 49516

© 1999 by Gary L. McIntosh

Published by Fleming H. Revell
a division of Baker Book House Company
P.O. Box 6287, Grand Rapids, MI 49516-6287

Fourth printing, January 2001

Printed in the United States of America

Library of Congress Cataloging-in-Publication Data

McIntosh, Gary, 1947–
    One size doesn't fit all : bringing out the best in any size church /
    Gary L. McIntosh.
       p.   cm.
    ISBN 0-8007-5699-1 (pbk.)
    1. Church growth. I. Title.
    BV652.25.M316 1999
    254—dc21   99–18717

For current information about all releases from Baker Book House, visit our web site:
http://www.bakerbooks.com

Dr. Win and Barbara Arn

Mentors who taught me
Friends who encourage me
Visionaries who will always inspire me

Contents

Acknowledgments

All books are to some extent a group project and *One Size Doesn't Fit All* is no exception. Thus my appreciation goes to the following who helped shape and form many of the insights woven throughout this book.

The pastors and congregations of the 500+ churches with whom I have consulted during the past 14 years

My friend and colleague at the Institute for American Church Growth (1983–1986) Rev. Robert Orr, who first introduced me to some of the ideas now fully developed in this book

The pastors who took time from their busy schedules to read the initial manuscript of this book and offer numerous affirmations and suggestions: Dr. Mahlon Friesen, Dr. Ted Martinez, Dr. J. Michael Broyles, Dr. Gil Stieglitz, Dr. John Shumate, Dr. Jerry Rueb, Dr. Michael Bradaric, Dr. Lorenzo V. Gonzalez, Dr. David H. McKinley, Dr. Mark Belokonny, Dr. Raleigh Galgan, and Dr. Hozell C. Francis

My administrative assistants at Talbot School of Theology who supported me while I spent time away from the office to complete this book: Mrs. Megan Gibson and Mrs. Cathy Jensen

My daughter-in-law Laura McIntosh for proofreading the initial rough draft of the manuscript

My editorial team at Fleming H. Revell: William J. Petersen, Mary L. Suggs, and others behind the scenes for their encouragement and professional development of this project

10

Introduction

THIS IS THE STORY of a frustrated pastor who has run out of ideas about how to encourage growth and spiritual development in his church. He seeks the counsel of a seasoned pastor and through the older man's wise mentoring learns that a church can flourish when the leaders remember that *One Size Doesn't Fit All*.

The ideas that the experienced pastor passes on to the younger man are concepts that I have developed through my study of church growth and my consultation experience with more than five hundred churches throughout the United States and Canada.

It is my hope that as you read this pastor's story and understand the concepts involved in *One Size Doesn't Fit All*, you will learn how to encourage growth in your own church and make disciples for our Lord Jesus Christ. What you learn here can give you and your church hope for the future.

This pastor's story is a compilation of stories that I have heard through my consultation experience. Any similarities between the characters and examples portrayed here and those of any person or church are purely coincidental.

1

What Size Are You?

MY STORY BEGINS SOME FIVE YEARS AGO. I was sitting in my church office looking out the window at my children playing in the parsonage driveway. Their innocent fun briefly diverted my attention from the frustrations I was feeling after only six months in the pastorate.

For eight years I had felt the calling of God to pastor a church. Seven years' experience in two different churches as a youth pastor and assistant pastor plus seminary training seemed like enough background to make me successful in ministry. Looking back, of course, I can see how much I did not know about effective ministry, but at the time I felt fairly confident I would do well.

The first three months went smoothly as my wife and I relocated into the spacious three-thousand-square-foot church parsonage, enrolled our children in the local elementary school, and acquainted ourselves with the city. Moving into my own office after four years of sharing a home office with our washer and dryer was a relief. The weekly routine of church ministry proved exhilarating. I enjoyed putting into practice the many skills I had acquired in seminary. Preparing sermons, teaching Bible studies, and administrating a church program fulfilled my dreams and calling. People responded well to my preaching, and enthusiastically I visited all the church members in the first three months of my pastorate. There were only thirty-five members, but the church appeared to have some potential, located only a couple blocks from a busy freeway.

This three-month "honeymoon" period gradually gave way to reality. My initial attempts to implement the programs I had successfully used in previous churches failed. As an example, I tried to begin an Evangelism Explosion ministry to reach people for Christ. However, we had a visitation list of only nineteen people. Our visitation teams visited all nineteen people, and one person even prayed to accept Christ. However, she never came to church. After exhausting our visitation list, the evangelism ministry collapsed due to the lack of people to contact. Our small church just did not have enough visitors to sustain a visitation-oriented style of evangelism.

I next looked to the Sunday school to see what might be done to build that ministry. Unfortunately the only children in the Sunday school were my own two children. The neighborhood around the church was changing from a residential area to an industrial area, and families did not see my church as a place to bring children. While I had successfully led a growing Sunday school program in a previous church, there was not much of a foundation to build on in this smaller church. Newer ideas for ministry, such as the creative "coffee house" style of ministry targeting local college students also fell through to my disappointment. People from the local college did not come, but that is a story for another time.

So there I sat, just six months into my first solo pastorate, struggling with the fact that I did not know how to lead this small church into renewed growth and vitality. The things I had learned in seminary—Christian education, biblical languages, homiletics, church history—while important foundations to my future ministry, had not provided me with the skills to lead this first small church.

That is why I called Bob Morrison. I had heard his name mentioned respectfully among pastors in my area. He had come to his present church directly out of seminary. That was twenty-nine years ago when Bob's church had only eight families. Remarkably he has seen the church grow through several stages of development. Today Bob preaches to nearly 1,750 people in three worship services on Sunday morning and a new worship service will be started on Saturday evenings in the fall. I had learned that Bob likes to mentor young pastors, which was exactly what I needed. So I gave him a call.

When we met for breakfast, my frustration must have shown on my face. After a few minutes of cordial conversation, Bob asked, "So, being a solo pastor of a small church isn't as easy as you thought, huh?"

"You can say that again," I answered. "The church members are friendly enough, but whatever I try to do seems to be ignored." I lamented the various failed programs I had tried to start in the last six months and told him how the same efforts had reaped fruit in another church where I had served.

Bob asked about my previous church experience, and I explained that while attending college I had accepted Christ in a church of about five hundred worshipers. After graduating, I became the youth pastor in the same church with responsibility for more than seventy-five students. Not wanting to make a short story too long, I shared how God had called me to seminary and that after seminary I had accepted a position as the assistant pastor in a church with about three hundred worshipers. My duties included overseeing the age-graded Sunday school, directing the junior and senior high youth ministry, and leading a highly successful neighborhood Vacation Bible School, which attracted more than two hundred children for two weeks annually.

Bob listened carefully to my story. When I finished, he affirmed my past experiences and asked me to tell him what made my present ministry so frustrating. "Well, I could give you several reasons," I moaned, "but here's an example that happened at my last board meeting."

Launching into a detailed account of the previous board meeting, I explained how I had wanted to challenge the board to greater vision. If I had learned anything about this church, it was that the people lacked a sense of vision. At one time, attendance at this church had averaged more than two hundred worshipers, but over a ten-year period, two church splits eroded the church membership down to the present thirty-five members. Those who remained retreated within to protect what church ministry was left. My previous ministry experience taught me that growing churches have vision, and it was clear my current small church did not have much. At one point in the meeting I challenged the board, "Let's dream a little about the future. Tell me where you want your church to be in twenty-five years."

The board members just sat in silence until Frank, an elderly member of the board, laughingly said, "Pastor, I'm not sure I'll be here in twenty-five years." Recognizing that twenty-five years was too great a time span for the board to envision, I suggested they tell where the church should be in ten years. However, that still seemed too much for them. "Five years?" I asked. Still no good ideas came forth. Finally, in a somewhat critical tone, I pleaded, "Okay, what do you think God wants us to do in the next year?"

Raising my voice and attracting the attention of the people in the next booth, I exploded, "Frankly, I'm a bit perplexed. The board even had a tough time thinking one year ahead. Don't these people know that without a vision the people perish?"

Bob had listened to me for quite a while, watching my body language and hearing my tone of voice. When I stopped talking, he offered his first bit of insight. He suggested that I appeared to be the victim of a fundamental misunderstanding and then he said:

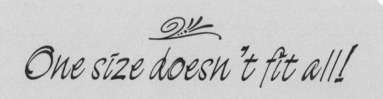

One size doesn't fit all!

Surprised by Bob's comment, I wondered out loud, "One size doesn't fit all? What do you mean?"

Bob began to explain, "It appears to me that you're trying to lead a small church like you would a larger church." Reaching into his briefcase, he pulled out a paper and laid it on the table between us. "Look at this breakdown of churches in the United States."

Attendance	Percentile
2000+	99%
800–1999	98%
400–799	95%
250–399	90%
200–249	85%
150–199	80%
140–149	75%
130–139	70%
100–129	60%
75–99	50%
55–74	40%
45–54	35%
40–44	30%
35–39	25%
30–34	20%
25–29	15%
20–24	10%
19 or less	5%

Bob explained that using worship attendance, rather than membership statistics, is generally thought to be more reliable for measuring church size. Then he clarified that the percentile column shows the percentage of churches smaller than the size indicated. For example, the 75th percentile means 75 percent of all churches have fewer than 149 worshipers on a Sunday morning. He then briefly summarized a few insights from the chart. First, Protestant churches vary a great deal in size. Second, most churches are fairly small with 50 percent of all churches under 100, and 80 percent under 200 in attendance on an average Sunday morning. Third, the remaining 20 percent of all churches are evenly divided between medium and large churches. According to the best estimates, 10 percent of churches are between 200 and 400 in size, with the remaining 10 percent more than 400. Fourth, less than 1 percent of all churches fall into the category of a mega church, having 2,000 or more worshipers.

While this chart of churches is interesting, Bob suggested that it is most helpful to think of churches as small, medium, and large. Turning over the piece of paper he scribbled the following on the back:

Small Church	Medium Church	Large Church
15–200	201–400	401+
80% of churches	10% of churches	10% of churches

"I never thought of a church of two hundred worshipers as being small," I commented.

"That's understandable," Bob agreed. "I use two hundred worshipers as the dividing line between small and medium churches because a major shift in a church's orientation takes place at that point. Churches with fewer than two hundred people attending worship exhibit a relational orientation. However, a church's orientation changes to more of a programmatical orientation as it grows beyond two hundred. It is a church's orientation that makes it small, medium, or large. I don't have time to explain the three main church orientations today. We'll talk more about them later."

"Okay," I said, "but I tend to think there's a great deal of difference between a church of 29 and one of 149."

"There are actually three levels of small church: small, smaller, and smallest," Bob explained. "The first level is comprised of churches averaging fewer than thirty-five worshipers on Sunday morning. Some people call this smallest church a chapel. The second level is comprised of churches averaging between thirty-six and seventy-five at worship. This smaller church is often referred to as a "typical" church in size. The third level is made up of churches between seventy-six and two hundred at worship. Depending on whom you read and what church association or denomination you are involved in, this size church may be viewed as a middle-sized church or even a large church. However, I call it a small church."

After sipping his coffee, Bob continued, "There are numerous ways to define different types of churches. For example, various categories often used are theological position, ethnic heritage, rural-urban orientation, growth or decline, health, worship style, and the age of the congregation. However, the most useful system is to group churches by size. Comparing churches by size reveals more helpful information for faithful ministry than looking at their denomination, location, or any of the other numerous methods of comparison."

When Bob stopped talking to take another drink of coffee, I challenged, "We can and do catalog churches in all these different ways, but what difference does it make? Churches are churches. In fact, I read a recent survey that indicated all churches have essentially the same problems regardless of their size."[1]

Bob disagreed sharply. He didn't dispute that there are some similarities among all churches but he said that for church leaders to be effective they must understand that churches have different needs depending on size. He further explained how a small church is not just a miniature version of a large church but an entirely different entity. What works for a church of one thousand is often not helpful to a church of four hundred or a church of thirty-five. Specific strategies for different size churches are necessary. Effective church leaders build on this fact. For instance, to help their churches grow, the Church of the Nazarene has designed Church Size Strategies for training church leaders. Under the creative leadership of Dr. Bill M. Sullivan, three church size strategies are in active operation: The Small Church Institute, The Intermediate Church Initiative, and The K-Church Project.[2] These strategies are built around the small, medium, and large breakdown. Bob explained that it is helpful to consider at least six implications of the value of categorizing churches.

1. For most congregations, church size is more important than the denominational label in planning for mission and ministry.
2. When a pastor moves from one church to another, a change in the size of the congregation often requires more adjustments on his part than is required by the change in geography.
3. Training seminars or workshops tend to be more productive if they bring together people based on church size rather than other criteria.
4. Efforts at cooperation among congregations are easier to implement among churches of the same size from different affiliations than among churches of different sizes from the same affiliation.
5. A change in size often causes feelings of insecurity, unrest, and frustration among members of the church.
6. The leaders of a congregation looking to learn from the experience of others will usually find it helpful to look to congregations of the same size, regardless of affiliation, rather than to limit themselves to churches in the same denomination or association.[3]

"What you're implying is that part of my problem is I'm employing large-church strategies in a small church. Is that correct?" As Bob nodded, he sent my thoughts back to my church. Perhaps a better understanding of the different sizes of churches could be helpful to my ministry. At least I would understand where to begin.

"Instead of applying a one-size-fits-all method to ministry, I need to adapt my approaches to the size of the church?"

"That's part of it," Bob answered, "but let's get back to my notes."

Picking up the sheet of paper on which he had been scribbling, Bob returned to his earlier thoughts. He recollected that in 1940 a man named William Sheldon had identified three basic body types—the thin person, the round person, and the classic person. He explained how most people have a little bit of each body type, but we all tend to resemble one type more than the others. In a similar manner, Bob suggested that there are three basic sizes of churches—small, medium, and large. While all churches resemble some aspects of all sizes of churches, each one demonstrates specific characteristics based on the category of size it falls into. Every church is different to some degree and these general size categories help us to understand why some move ahead and others falter. Churches seem to go through similar phases based on their size.

"You want another refill on those coffees?" interrupted our waitress.

"No, but give me the check," I said. "I've got to pay for this free consultation somehow." Graciously Bob accepted my offer to pay for his meal, then suggested what I had hoped to hear. He noted that we had just scratched the surface in our discussion about church sizes and wondered if we could get together for breakfast the next week.

"I was hoping we could talk some more about this issue. You've given me some new ideas to think about, but I'm sure there is more."

"Yes!" Bob added, "In fact let's put this breakfast meeting on our calendars for the next ten weeks! I want to develop this idea of church size completely for you by comparing the differences between small, medium, and large churches and by answering the following questions:

What is the church's orientation?
How is the church structured?
Who sets the direction?
What is the pastor's role?
How are decisions made?
What is the impact of staff?
How does change take place?
How do churches grow?
What are the obstacles to growth?
What are the strategies for growth?"

"Sounds good to me!" I pushed my plate away, retrieved my calendar, and placed it on the table in front of me. "I'm going to write these dates in ink rather than in pencil."

"Just two more things," Bob requested. "First, do me a favor this week and spend some time observing how your current church is different from medium- and larger-sized churches. Make a short list and bring it with you next week. If you do, I'll pay for breakfast. Second, let me pray for you before we go."

Taking It Home

I picked up the papers on which Bob had scribbled so I could read and think about them during the week. By the time I reached the church, I had thought of several differences between small, medium, and large churches. How many differences can you list?

Small Church	Medium Church	Large Church
15–200	201–400	401+
80% of churches	10% of churches	10% of churches

1.

2.

3.

4.

5.

6.

7.

What Is the Church's Orientation?

ALL WEEK I HAD BEEN THINKING about the lesson I had learned from Bob—one size doesn't fit all. The more I pondered this insight, running it through my grid of past ministry experiences, the more it made sense. Driving the five miles from my home to the restaurant where we were to meet, I reflected on my mental list of the differences between small, medium, and large churches. I looked forward to spending more time with Bob, wondering what new ideas would be gained from the morning's meeting. As I drove into the parking lot, I spotted Bob entering the restaurant. By the time I parked my car and walked in, he had secured a table for us. Pulling his chair away from the table, Bob jokingly asked, "Who's paying for breakfast today?"

"You are," I joked in return. "I did my assignment just as you requested."

We ordered our meals, and then Bob asked to see my list. I confessed that most of my ideas were in my mind but that I had jotted down a few thoughts. Removing a page from my notebook, I handed him the following list:

Small Church	Medium Church	Large Church
Know all people	Know some people	Know few people
Meals a family affair	Meals a program affair	Meals a large-group affair
Extended family	Growing family	Multiple families

"This is a great start," Bob encouraged. "Why don't you briefly explain to me what these mean."

I began describing my list by noting that the first difference between churches of different sizes is in the number of people one knows face-to-face. One of the comforts and pleasures of a small church is that one can know everyone in the church. Then as the church grows and becomes more complex, fewer people are known on a first-name basis. By the time a church is large, it is rare to know anyone outside one's own ministry or fellowship group.

I explained that this change in personal relationships is demonstrated in the way church meals are handled. For example, in a small church meals are often a family affair, with each family bringing something to add to a potluck. The small church needs no reason to have a meal together other than fellowship. Eating together *is* the reason for gathering, just as it is in a family.

In contrast, meals in a medium church are often held as reinforcement for an ongoing program within the church—the reason people eat a meal together is not primarily for fellowship, but to reinforce some other aspect of ministry, such as planning for Sunday school or assimilating newcomers. As a result, only a fraction of the total membership gather, rather than the entire church. My guess to Bob was that those gathered for a meal in a medium church comprise only about 5 percent of the total church.

Meals in the large church facilitate larger group events, such as a fund-raising banquet or an evangelistic outreach. Such meals are not potlucks but in many cases are catered. I shared with Bob that this all could be summarized in the last comparison: extended family, growing family, and multiple families. The smaller church seems to be one large family, while the large church is a complex gathering of multiple families. Medium churches are extended families in the process of growing into multiple families.

All the time I talked, Bob confirmed my discoveries with occasional interjections such as "I see," "Go on," "You're right." As we continued our breakfast, Bob suggested that the central question to ask about churches of various sizes is:

What is the church's orientation?

As Bob began to talk, I took out a pad of paper and started taking notes. "All churches have a central organizing principle or orientation," Bob declared. "In the small church, the organizing principle is a *relational orientation*. Another way to describe it is a *familial orientation*. One needs to think of the small church as a very large or extended family. When the church meets, there is a feeling of kinship. Each person knows all the others. Churchwide gatherings that include a meal are much like family reunions. Dinners held for families following a funeral, for the annual Sunday school picnic, or to celebrate a couple's fiftieth wedding anniversary enhance the feeling of family ties."

Bob gave an example of this personal family orientation with a poem that I can quote word for word to this day.

> In a big world,
> the small church has remained intimate.
> In a fast world,
> the small church has been steady.
> In an expensive world,
> the small church has remained plain.
> In a complex world,
> the small church has remained simple.
> In a rational world,
> the small church has kept feeling.
> In a mobile world,
> the small church has been an anchor.
> In an anonymous world,
> the small church calls us by name.[4]

I have since discovered that in many small churches a rich history of ministry, devotion, and sacrifice can be attributed to the personal nature of this family orientation. One pastor put it this way:

> In a small church you know the members—their names, their families, their interests, their work places. When you preach to the people you are not preaching to a sea of unknown faces but to familiar faces. Your sermons are not a general scattering of words hoping to hit some unknown target. Your sermons can be directed to real problems and needs you know exist.
> In a small church, you can minister to the people at deep levels of relationships. A small church often is characterized by intimacy.[5]

Anyone who has spent time in a small church recognizes the reality of the relational orientation found there. Many, if not most, small churches place a high premium on relationships. Preferences, decisions, choices, judgments, elections, conclusions, resolutions, and votes are influenced by this organizing principle.

"By contrast," continued Bob, "the central organizing principle of a medium church may be described as a *programmatical orientation.* The medium church actually functions as a collection of family groups—classes, circles, fellowships, clubs, or organizations—rather than an extended family group. In some cases the medium-sized church is simply an overgrown small church, but a true medium-sized church is a complex mixture of numerous influential groups. The expansion of the medium church into various groups is normally accompanied by corresponding programs or ministries identified with these groups. The youth are tied to a youth ministry, the women to a women's ministry, the young marrieds to a young marrieds' Sunday school class, seniors to a seniors' program, and so forth. The organizing principle is no longer one of relationships, as connected to the extended family; rather, the organizing principle is the programmatical orientation attached to the various groups. Influence on decisions is driven by what will perpetuate the program rather than what will be acceptable to the family."

"You're right," I responded. "When I was an assistant pastor in a church of three hundred worshipers, it seemed as though everything was driven by the church program. The church I'm in now cares little about any program. One of their favorite sayings is 'People are more important than programs.' What you're saying makes a lot of sense."

Bob went on. "To continue my comparison, the best way to conceptualize the large church is, as well-known parish consultant Lyle Schaller suggests, a congregation of congregations.[6] When the groups found in the medium church grow larger, they actually take on the characteristic of small churches within a single large church, thus a congregation of congregations. The larger number of church participants within one church creates the need for additional structure and organized group life to maintain the health and vitality of the large church. This leads to a central organizing principle in the large church that can best be termed an *organizational orientation.*

Briefly stated the small church functions as a big happy family, the medium church as a collection of subgroups, and the large church as an organization."

"I like the way you're comparing the central organizing principles of different size churches," I interrupted. "When I served as youth pastor in a church of five hundred people, I observed the reality of the congregation of congregations phenomenon in the frequently heard references to 'The crowd at the early service' or 'The nine o'clock congregation.' Looking back, it's clear that the church was a congregation of congregations."

In my notes I wrote the following:

The Church's Orientation
or
Central Organizing Principle

Small Church	Medium Church	Large Church
Relational	Programmatical	Organizational

Looking at Bob, I said, "This really hits home. It's apparent that in attempting to replicate my past experience in my present church, I've totally ignored my church's central organizing principle."

"That's true," Bob confirmed. "Your focus on designing programs is fine for a medium-sized church but misses the mark for a small church. And the manner in which you challenged the board to increase their vision was appropriate for a large church but again didn't hit home with your smaller relational church. Now don't misunderstand me," Bob cautioned. "Programs and vision are crucial needs but they must be approached relationally in the smaller church."

"I'm beginning to see that," I interjected. "Reflecting on this major question helps put things into perspective."

"It sure does," smiled Bob. "Let's dig a little deeper into this thought. I recall a concept often used by Carl Dudley, a leading expert on smaller-sized churches. He suggests there are two types of communities—the relational community and the rigorous community. These correspond roughly to the small church and the large church.

"In the relational community a group consciousness or spirit defines the individuals. It provides a framework of values, beliefs, and commitments against which the members measure their lives. The church knows who it is because it has a communal consciousness supported by family, history, and land. The group determines its identity from its past, which is carried on by tradition with a certain rhythm and sense of permanence. In a sense, the past is always present. Thus words like *change* and *creativity* are enemies, since the church cannot imagine doing things differently. Its goal is not so much to change the world as it is to know each other better.

"In the rigorous community the individuals are connected to each other by a collection of contracts for a common end. Vision and plans are embraced as members define their values based on their common productivity and success in reaching the community's goals. Their identity is determined more by the future than the past. Thus words like *change* and *creativity* challenge them to attempt greater things for God. Their goal is to do their share to build God's kingdom."[7]

"That's a valuable distinction to make," I offered. "In my present dilemma I can see I'm a rigorous community person trying to lead a relational community. But what about the medium-sized church? Where does it fit?"

Bob reached for my notepad and pulled out his pen. After drawing the following picture, he pressed on.

"From my observations of churches over the past twenty-nine years, it appears to me that some, but certainly not all, medium-sized churches are transitional in nature."

"What do you mean by 'transitional'?"

Pointing to the drawing he had just made, Bob remarked, "On the left side is the small church, or what I've been describing as a relational community. Research gathered by Lyle Schaller suggests that small is the normative size of Protestant congregations in America. His study confirms that 'the small church, with fewer than 100

Small

Large

Med

31

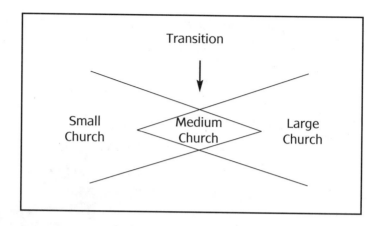

worshipers on the typical weekend, is the norm in American Protestantism. Approximately three out of five of all congregations fit into that size bracket."[8] This matches nicely with the chart I gave you last week, even though I'm using a broader definition for a small church. The main fact is small churches are the norm."

"I get the picture. Wherever I drive around town, I see many small churches. Yet it seems like all we hear and read about are the larger ones."

"That's to be expected," Bob said. "Small churches may be the norm, but it's the number of large churches that is growing. That number has at least quadrupled since the 1950s and that's news. Since most church growth has occurred in churches of more than three hundred in size, it's not surprising that research and reports have been done on them. We all want to see our churches grow. At least I've never heard of any church leader who honestly wanted his church to decline. It's significant that larger churches seem to attract a large population of people born after 1955. At least one-half of the post-1955 generation who attend church can be found in the top 10 percent of churches."

"Okay, so small churches are the norm and large churches are growing. Where do the medium-sized churches fit in?"

"Well, the numbers of both smaller churches and larger churches are increasing, but the proportion of medium-sized churches is declining.[9] Essentially it appears that to some extent the medium-sized church is in a transitional phase. All large churches were small at one time and grew from small to medium to large. So it's obvious that a certain percentage of churches make it through this transitional phase. However, after several years of numerical growth, many medium-sized churches face the decision of having to adjust their ministries to continue growing into a large church. If they don't make the appropriate adjustments, they will either plateau for a time or decline back to a small church size. Some medium-sized churches will plateau and stay at the medium church size, but the pull downward is stronger than the pull upward. It's usually just a matter of time before the plateaued church gets smaller."

"Let me have that pad of paper back for a minute," I said to Bob. He pushed it across the table and I added to the diagram.

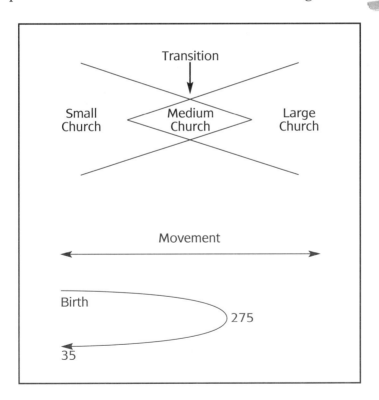

"I get the impression that a church can move back and forth from one size to another. Is that correct?" I questioned.

"Absolutely," Bob replied. "That first line shows the concept of movement well. What's the second line?"

"That's the history of my current church. About thirty years ago the church was birthed by a small group of people who dreamed about starting a work for God in our community. It took nearly twenty years, but the church eventually reached a peak of 275 worship attenders. They faced some disagreement about whether to make the necessary adjustments to move on to become a large church, and a vote was taken. Using your terminology, the relational community won out over the rigorous community, and a split took place. Those in the relational community rejoiced in the belief they had protected the basic relational character of the small church. Those in the rigorous community decried the loss of vision and claimed the church was moving backward. After a few years the church suffered a second split and gradually declined back to a small church of thirty-five members. It's a classic case."

"This is sad. At first glance it appears that your church experienced a common occurrence among medium-sized churches. Quite a number of churches that find themselves in the medium-sized zone are in an awkward situation that I call a *stretched cell.* I want to talk to you more about this next time we meet."

"Same time? Same place?" I asked.

"Sounds good."

"And don't forget," I reminded him, "you're buying today."

Taking It Home

Once during the week, I woke up at two o'clock in the morning thinking about the central organizing principles of the three sizes of churches. I often wake up like this after my subconscious mind has worked on a newly acquired insight. It has been my practice to keep a notepad on the nightstand by my bed to jot down my late-night ideas. This night I began to list the ways that I had observed the central organizing principles operating in various sized churches. See how many ideas you can add to my list.

The Church's Orientation
or
Central Organizing Principle

Small Church	Medium Church	Large Church
Relational	*Programmatical*	*Organizational*
1. Workday attended by entire church.	Men's group organizes and supports workday.	Private contractors hired to do the work.
2. Church Christmas party for all members.	Christmas parties for groups and classes.	Numerous Christmas parties planned.
3. Past is important.	Present is important.	Future is important.
4.		
5.		
6.		
7.		

How Is the
Church Structured?

My wife and I always reserve Monday night as a family night. Evenings tend to fill up with church events, and I have realized that meetings shove family time aside if I let them. We have discovered the most efficient way to be with the family is to schedule one evening a week together, which we have done for about three years.

On this Monday evening, it was difficult to keep my mind on playtime with my children. The discussions I had had with Bob kept creeping back into my thoughts. At one point in the evening my five-year-old daughter climbed into my lap with her favorite toy—a kaleidoscope. She loves to hold it up to a light and turn it ever so slightly to see the changing pictures. Eventually she lifted it up to my face and I took a turn peering through the small opening. As I scanned the intricate patterns created in the kaleidoscope, my mind skipped back to Bob's discussion of small, medium, and large churches. Viewing churches through Bob's eyes was similar to gazing at them through a kaleidoscope. I was seeing a completely new picture. Each time we met, I developed a different perception and awareness of churches.

The next time we met together Bob presented me with a card labeled *McIntosh's Typology of Church Sizes.* The card summarized the differences in church sizes to which Bob was introducing me. The first three factors on the card summarized where Bob and I were in our discussions.

McIntosh's Typology of Church Sizes

Factors	Small Church	Medium Church	Large Church
Size	15–200 worshipers	201–400 worshipers	401+ worshipers
Orientation	Relational	Programmatical	Organizational
Structure	Single cell	Stretched cell	Multiple cell

"How do you know so much about church sizes?" I asked.

"Well," he explained, "I have been observing churches for a number of years. But one day a brochure came in the mail advertising a church growth seminar. At first I was a little skeptical since I'd attended my share of seminars that weren't very helpful."

"Me too!" I agreed.

"At the time, the church I pastored had plateaued. We were a medium-sized church that got stuck on the way to becoming a large church and I couldn't understand why. Grasping for any insights that would help me, I decided to attend. The training event was taught by its creator, Dr. Gary L. McIntosh, and the take-home values were top-notch. It was a blessing I attended because it was there I learned about stretched cells."

"Yes! What are stretched cells? You said we'd talk about them today."

"We actually need to discuss the entire concept of church structure," Bob said and forged ahead while I eagerly took notes.

Bob explained how, when one attempts to define *small, medium,* and *large* as they relate to church size, it is natural to think of numbers. However, he suggested that it is better to define churches as *single cell, stretched cell,* and *multiple cell.* Small churches tend to be single cell, medium churches often are stretched cells, and large churches are multiple cells.

"I'll never forget one of the stories McIntosh told at the seminar," Bob went on. "He told us how he had visited a church in Iowa as a candidate for director of Christian education. After preaching in one of the services, he stood at the front door greeting people as they were leaving.

"McIntosh shared that many of the people mentioned that they were related to others in the church. It seemed that nearly everyone was related biologically or by marriage. The entire church of nearly 250 people was an interesting mixture of cousins, aunts, uncles, children, parents, and grandparents."

Bob obviously enjoyed retelling this story. He explained that this church was clearly a single cell church. While most single cell churches are those with a small membership or attendance, single cells may be found in larger churches also. This was the case of the church McIntosh had talked about. Numerically the church was a medium-sized church but structurally it was a small church—single cell.

Then Bob defined *single cell* churches as those that have three major characteristics:

1. They have a close, face-to-face fellowship.
2. They have one or two families at the center of the church.
3. They have the feeling of being a large, loving family.

According to Bob, "Single cell churches enjoy a close, face-to-face relationship in which everyone knows everyone else in the church. Their fellowship extends beyond Sunday morning as they relate to each other in the community through numerous activities. Values, style, history, memories, and concerns are commonly held together.

"Decision-making power normally resides in one or two families whose family members regularly hold the key ministry positions in the church. A strong sense of faith, loyalty, and pride permeates the key families. It is their stubborn courage against change that keeps the church committed to traditions.

"The feeling of being a large loving family is expressed through love and care for members of the church family. Any church member experiencing a crisis, pain, or struggle can count on the church family to support him or her in or outside the church."

When Bob finished giving these details about single cell churches, he drew the following diagram to picture a single cell church.

Bob commented on the drawing: "This diagram depicts the internal structure of a single cell church. Note that all programs

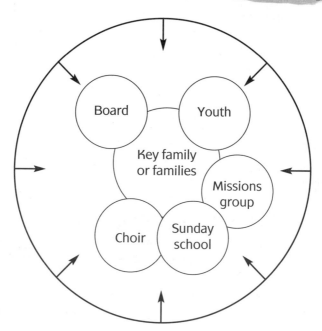

and ministries are connected to the key family or families. The members may belong to any or all of the groups but they all make up a single fellowship or family. Decision-making administrative boards draw most of their members from the key families, which allows these families to maintain a measure of control over the entire church. Note that the central focus of the church, indicated by the arrows, is internal on the needs, cares, concerns, and interests of the single cell.

Bob pointed out that newcomers find it difficult to become accepted unless they meet one of the following criteria:

1. They are born into one of the key families.
2. They marry someone from one of the key families.
3. They have a gregarious personality.
4. They have something of value to offer that the church needs, such as talents, spiritual gifts, money, or prestige.
5. They experience a crisis along with the key families.

"Stop for just a second," I interrupted. "It's clear to me I'm in a single cell church. What does a stretched cell church look like?"

"Bear with me for a few minutes. I'd like to move on to the multiple cell church, and then we'll come back to the stretched cell." Taking his yellow pad, Bob sketched the following diagram.

"This is a multiple cell church," he said. "There are people in the church who are formal members and many who are not. Yet there are so many people that it is impractical to expect any single person to know everyone else. Church attenders are involved in a number of small and large groups with most having little or no regular contact with each other. Rather than being one large, loving family, the multiple cell church is a collection of families, a congregation of congregations. It is in these small cells that people are known, loved, cared for, and supported through times of crisis. Also there is a balanced focus both outward and inward. See the arrows pointing in and out? This does not normally exist in a single cell church. Newcomers sense that it is easier to become involved in a multiple

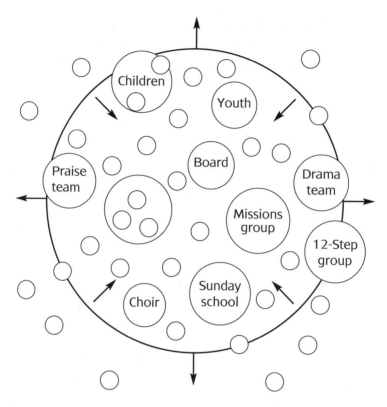

cell church than in a single cell church, in part due to the many group opportunities that are available."

Bob listed the characteristics of a *multiple cell* church:

1. There are too many people to know everyone.
2. There are numerous groups, classes, and cells where people can become involved. The church is a congregation of congregations.
3. Church leadership is representative of several groups, classes, and cells.

"It's crucial to understand that the decision-making power doesn't reside in one or two families. We'll talk about the leadership of each size church later, but for now jot down in your notes that the main administrative board is comprised of people from various cells rather than from just one, as it is in a single cell church. The makeup of the leadership is a key factor that shows the contrast between a single cell church and a multiple cell church.

"With the single cell and multiple cell church in mind, let's think about the stretched cell," Bob said as he once again drew on his legal pad.

"Remember I mentioned last week that in some cases the medium church is in a transitional phase between the small and large church?"

"Yes," I nodded. "You said that the medium-sized church is in somewhat of an awkward stage of transition."

"You have a good memory. Here is a stretched cell," he said, pointing to his diagram.

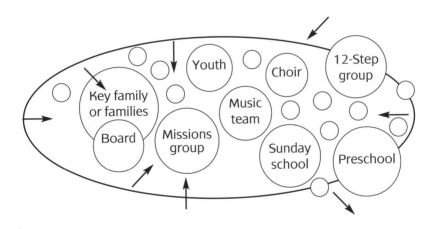

"What you're looking at is a medium church that started as a small church and has experienced strong growth. What jumps out at you?"

Looking closely at Bob's diagram, I ventured to guess: "The main ministries that were found in the small church—choir, missions, Sunday school, and others—are still in place. Yet some other ministries have been added, such as the 12-Step group, the music team, and the preschool."

"That's correct. It's a good guess that the growth in the church can be directly related to the new ministries. The addition of new groups, classes, and ministries normally opens the door for newcomers to find a way into a church.

"What else do you see?" Bob pressed me to look more closely at the drawing.

"I'm not sure what you want me to see," I stammered.

"Don't miss the fact that the key families are still in place, and ..."

"Oh, I see it now!" I blurted out. "The key families are still there *and* they are still in control of the church."

"You've got it!" Bob seemed to enjoy the fact that I had discovered the key characteristic of a stretched cell. He noted, "It's interesting, isn't it, that the church has grown numerically from a small church to a medium-sized church, but the same families continue to be in charge. A stretched cell is a church that has grown numerically large enough to be considered a medium church but has not added new leadership to its governing board. The church is too large to be considered a small church but is not quite large enough to be a multiple cell church. A true multiple cell church derives its leadership from different cells. The stretched cell church is larger but still finds its leadership in only one cell—the former single cell members."

In my notebook I summarized the characteristics of a *stretched cell* church:

1. The church is of medium size.
2. New programs and ministries are effective in bringing newcomers into the church.
3. The leadership continues to be drawn almost completely from the original families in the church.

"This is all interesting, but what are the implications?" I asked.

"The main implication," Bob offered, "is that the church is in danger of moving back to being a small church. It's like this rubber band I'm holding. Let's pretend that this loose rubber band is a small church. One day a visionary pastor or group of laypersons begins to establish a few new ministries. The newer ministries begin to draw new people into the church, which causes the church to grow or expand like when I pull the rubber band out. The church is stretched like this rubber band is now. To keep the rubber band stretched, I have to keep exerting pressure or it'll contract back to a smaller size. In a stretched cell, some person, group of persons, or ministry acts as a catalyst (or pressure), stretching the church larger. As long as the catalyst remains in place, the church keeps growing. If, however, it is removed, such as when a pastor leaves or a new ministry is discontinued, the church goes back down in size. In most situations once a church has been stretched larger, it doesn't go back to its original size but it does shrink a great deal.

"When I attended the seminar I mentioned earlier, McIntosh told a story that is a good example of what happens with a stretched cell.

"McIntosh shared that a good friend of his became the pastor of a small church with a worship attendance of approximately eighty-five persons. The governing board consisted of three people—two people from the key family in the church and the newly arrived pastor. Over the next four years the church grew to an average worship attendance of three hundred persons! A number of changes contributed to the church's growth. A new children's program was started, attracting nearly 150 children to a weeknight event. Several families became acquainted with the church through the children's program and eventually joined the church. The pastor began preaching with a more relational style, which included dressing casually, moving away from the pulpit to walk among the people, and preaching without notes. During this same four-year period, a new contemporary style of music was incorporated on Sunday mornings.

"All these factors resulted in a worship attendance growth of an additional 215 persons in a four-year period. Unfortunately the governing board added only one additional person to its membership during that same period. The board fought hard to return the church to its previous small church size by resisting the development of new ministries and vetoing creative ideas brought to them by the pastor. This church was a classic example of a stretched cell. The church had grown, but the administrative board had essentially remained the same. Eventually McIntosh's friend left the church, and within one year it had dropped down to about 125 worshipers. It didn't quite go back to 85 people but it didn't remain a medium church either."

"Are all medium-sized churches stretched cells?" I inquired.

"No, the key is to look at the leadership in the church. If the leaders of a medium church continue to represent only the former families from the church's smaller days, then it is a stretched cell. If, however, the leaders represent several of the newer cells and newer members, it has actually become a medium-sized church. It also stands a good chance of becoming a large church."

"I'll bet I know the name of the seminar you attended," I said. "One Size Doesn't Fit All."

"How did you guess?" Bob asked, grinning.

Taking It Home

I already knew the church I pastored was a single cell church, but Bob gave me a questionnaire to help me know for sure. Now you can determine if your church is a single cell, stretched cell, or multiple cell. Check the statements that seem to describe your church the best.

_____ 1. Most persons in my church know each other by name and have several opportunities to make contact beyond church.

_____ 2. Persons in my church know quite a few members but by no means all; there are a few opportunities to make contact outside of church.

_____ 3. Persons in my church know very few members beyond their class or particular group; they have almost no contact outside of church.

_____ 4. Most members of my church live near the church building or within easy driving distance. Most live in the same community or share a common geographical identity.

_____ 5. Some members live near my church and others live some distance away. A few people drive to church from other communities and pass several other churches along the way.

_____ 6. Few members live near my church and most drive in from other communities, passing lots of other churches. A large number of the members identify with communities other than where the church is located.

_____ 7. The church sees itself as an extended family where many people are related or have been friends for many years.

_____ 8. The church has experienced growth as newcomers have joined, but the leadership core of the church still comes predominantly from a few key families or individuals.

_____ 9. The church is composed of persons who have few family ties to other members, and the leadership core represents a broad range of people and groups within the church.

_____ 10. There are regular meals held for the entire church to celebrate friendship and family ties to other members.

_____ 11. There are meals held primarily for select groups in the church to plan, conduct business, or introduce newcomers to the church.

_____ 12. There is an occasional meal, which is usually catered, held around large events for introducing new directions, such as building programs, or to honor people, such as volunteers.

_____ 13. A few key people seem to hold most of the leadership positions, and decisions appear to be made somewhat informally.

_____ 14. There are many newcomers working as volunteers or leading programs, but the core administrative board continues to be comprised of long-term trusted members; decisions seem to be made in committees or commissions.

_____ 15. Leadership roles are distributed among many persons who represent several different groups in the church;

47

decisions are made in formal settings, such as board meetings.

_____ 16. Church workdays or projects are completed by the entire church, and a representative of each family is almost always on hand.

_____ 17. Church projects are completed by small groups of persons but do not usually involve the entire church.

_____ 18. Church projects are completed by paid personnel or by outside contractors.

While there are always exceptions, numbers 1, 4, 7, 10, 13, and 16 tend to be true of *single cell* churches. Numbers 2, 5, 8, 11, 14, and 17 tend to be true of *stretched cell* churches. Numbers 3, 6, 9, 12, 15, and 18 tend to be true of *multiple cell* churches.

Occasionally churches find they are a complex mixture of all three types of churches, which normally points to a church in transition from one type to another.

What type of church does yours appear to be?

4

Who Sets the Direction?

THE SURVEY BOB GAVE ME as we walked out of the restaurant last week confirmed the fact that I was serving a single cell church. His ideas on how the leadership structure of a church resulted in some churches that were numerically medium size becoming stretched cells intrigued me. So, at our next meeting, I determined to arrive a short time before Bob in order to spend some quiet moments rethinking our previous week's discussion.

Pulling out the card on *McIntosh's Typology of Church Sizes,* I reviewed the list, stopping at the topic Bob and I were going to discuss that day—leadership.

My mind was so involved in meditating on the differences listed under "Leadership" that I did not notice Bob had arrived, until he spoke.

"How long have you been here?" Bob quizzed while taking his seat across from me in the booth.

McIntosh's Typology of Church Sizes

Factors	Small Church	Medium Church	Large Church
Size	15–200 worshipers	201–400 worshipers	401+ worshipers
Orientation	Relational	Programmatical	Organizational
Structure	Single cell	Stretched cell	Multiple cell
Leadership	Resides in key families	Resides in committees	Resides in select leaders

"Only about fifteen minutes," I confided. "I had some extra time and wanted to think about our last discussion."

"That's good. Anything in particular that's been on your mind?"

"I've been thinking about the place of leadership in my church and particularly how to assimilate new leaders so that we don't become a stretched cell."

By now I realized that Bob could not talk without drawing some pictures. It did not surprise me that he took a napkin and drew a diagram on it.

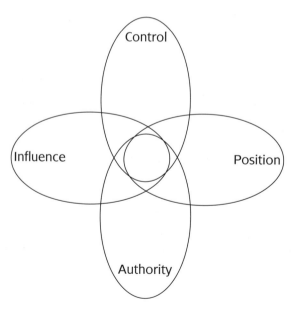

"From my viewpoint," Bob began, "effective leadership is made up of four ingredients: position, authority, influence, and control." He pointed to the diagram as he explained each aspect of leadership.

"The first ingredient of leadership is *position*. In every church a person or group of persons is perceived by the congregation as responsible for getting the job done. Those who are in leadership ultimately will be blamed when things fall apart and praised when things go well. These leaders are usually found on the main policy-making board of the church, but not always.

"*Authority*, which is the second ingredient, is the power to decide. The most basic authority is the power to say yes or no. Rarely does any one person or group have sole authority in every situation, but it does happen occasionally. Decision-making power in most situations is held in limited jurisdiction; for example, a youth pastor may have authority over the youth room at church but might need to ask for permission to use the fellowship hall.

"Another ingredient is *influence*. To lead others, an individual or group must be able to sway people to follow a proposed direction. The ability to command a following indicates one has the power of influence. A few years ago I heard Fred Roach, president of the Leadership Dynamics Institute at the Baylor Health Care System in Dallas, use this idea in his definition of a leader: 'a person who influences people to accomplish a purpose.'[10]

"The final ingredient is *control*. This aspect of leadership refers to the ability to get something accomplished. Effective leaders have the muscle, punch, or oomph to get the job done. Leaders don't just talk about doing something. They do it.

"Integrated together, these ingredients can be viewed as *leadership power:* the power of position, authority, influence, and control."

Feeling uncomfortable I broke in. "Bob, I feel a little uneasy with the use of the word *power*. Is it wise to use this term?"

"Please don't misunderstand me," Bob explained. "I'm not talking about evil or unwarranted power. I think you'll agree, however, that someone must set direction, make decisions, organize support, cast vision, and set the agenda in a church. I remember reading that

Time magazine once asked the question about our nation, 'Who's in charge?' *Time* supplied its own answer: 'The nation calls for leadership, and there is no one home.'[11] Someone must be home in the church. Another way to put this is to ask, Who sets the direction?"

Bob persisted, "Have you ever experienced a situation in which you've been given responsibility and yet you couldn't get anything accomplished because you didn't have any authority?"

"Yes, I'm actually in that situation right now. The church I'm serving wants me to lead them into renewed vitality but they withhold decision-making power. I have the position, or as you say, responsibility, to lead but almost no authority, influence, or control."

"Precisely," Bob jumped in. "We'll talk specifically about the leadership role of the pastor later on, but when it comes to the leadership of a church, it's wise to ask and answer the question, Who's in charge here?"

"Where does the issue of character fit into leadership power?" I questioned. "It seems that your diagram leaves out the character qualities found in First Timothy 3."

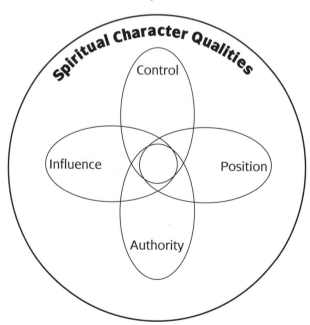

"I can see how you'd perceive that from this quick drawing," Bob agreed. "The spiritual character qualities actually undergird leadership power. Without character, there will be no spiritual power. Perhaps a circle around the illustration will show this." It is the spiritual character of the leader that empowers the four ingredients of leadership power.

"One more thought before we discuss leadership in the different size churches. Dynamic leadership occurs when all four of these ingredients of leadership coalesce. If all the ingredients of leadership come together in a single person or group, there is great leadership potential."

Bob drew the following diagram to illustrate coalesced leadership:

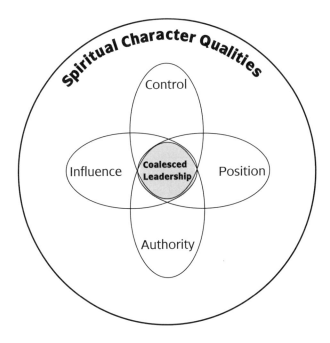

"Now, going back to our larger discussion, let's ask, Where does leadership power reside in each church size?"

Hardly taking a breath, Bob spelled out how this understanding of leadership power fit into our dialogue of different size churches.

Our conversation that day turned into an extended time that I will summarize briefly.

According to Bob, in the majority of cases, leadership power coalesces in a few key families in the small church. In general, the smaller church will find that members of its official governing board will come disproportionately from long-term members and one or two families within the church.

My church is a classic example of what Bob was explaining. Of the thirty-five members in my church, eleven are on the governing board. All eleven are long-term members with an average tenure of more than fifteen years. Seven of the board members are related to the two main families in the church while the remaining four are close friends of the key families. The members of the governing board have all the ingredients of leadership power: position, influence, authority, and control. I minister from the leadership position of pastor, but if I am to get anything accomplished, it is clear that I will need the key families to lead the way.

Another aspect of leadership power found in many small churches revolves around the personalities of the people Bob called the initiating leader, the patriarch, and the matriarch. Within the key families of the small church, one person can usually initiate new direction with the blessing of the family. In my church, as an example once again, this person happens to be the son of the patriarch and matriarch. If he suggests a new direction for the church, it is accepted. The patriarch and matriarch are the oldest couple in my church, and they also happen to be the heads of the main family in the church. Their role appears to be to remind everyone of the history and traditions of the church. I discovered quickly that nothing gets accomplished without their blessing. That is the reason, of course, their son can get away with being an initiating leader.

It's interesting that, with all the leadership power the governing boards have in small churches, they do not use it to move the church forward. Rather, they normally assume that the purpose of their leadership is to tell people, including the pastor, what they cannot do. As you have probably discovered for yourself at some time, having ideas turned down by the veto power of a board can be extremely frustrating.

Moving on, Bob emphasized that an interesting transition occurs when a church moves from a small church to a medium church. Leadership power moves away from key families and coalesces in major committees. The actual term for these groups may vary from church to church, but whatever the name—committee, commission, task force, or team—a similar pattern takes place. When the small church starts growing into a medium church, members and friends of the key families transition into service on program committees such as education, missions, nominating committee, trustees, worship, and finance. Through this means, often not recognized or acknowledged, the main families are able to maintain a measure of control even as the church grows.

Bob gave an illustration from his own ministry of how this happens. Here is his story:

"Our church grew from 75 worshipers to about 280 in the span of five years. The appearance of new faces on Sunday morning elicited joy and excitement from all. God had answered our prayer for growth, and we were elated. I thought we were on our way, but our growth stalled out and fluctuated around 250 to 280, except on special Sundays like Easter.

"I agonized over what was holding us back. It soon dawned on me that we weren't adding new leaders to our boards and committees. After making a list of our leaders, it was obvious that the same individuals from the same families, who held leadership power when the church was smaller, were still in control.

"Granted, they were no longer on the same board together but they had managed to move into trusted positions on various boards and committees. The matriarch served as Sunday school superintendent, the patriarch ministered as a deacon, their son was church treasurer, his wife was president of the women's group, and a cousin was chairperson of the elder board.

"They all maintained ministry positions within the church that allowed them an amazing amount of control. There was an appearance of new leadership development along with an unrecognized and unacknowledged control by long-term leaders.

"All my efforts to expand the leadership power to others was thwarted by decisions from these power people in the church."

Bob reiterated, "If the main families continue to be in control of the various boards and committees, the church becomes a stretched cell. If new leaders are assimilated into the numerous boards and committees, then the church moves forward and truly becomes a medium-sized church."

Bob further suggested that by the time a medium church progresses into a large church, the leadership power coalesces in the elected leaders. Leaders in large churches are most often chosen based on their abilities, skills, and gifts rather than their blood lines. Elected leaders in the large church serve where you would expect them to serve—on the governing board, finance or budget committee, personnel committee, or in offices such as president or moderator. While leaders in the large church tend to be selected from several different cells or family groups, rather than a few, there still continues to be a hierarchy of leadership rarely openly identified. Larger churches are disposed to elect their leaders from longer-term members, men, members over forty years old, those with high verbal skills, those engaged in business or professions, and those with previous leadership experience.

What started out as a short meeting turned into a rather long one. Once again I was surprised by the insights I had gained by listening to Bob expound on his experiences and insights regarding leadership in different size churches. Glancing away from Bob, I thought about the implication of his analysis on my own situation.

"Well? What do you think about all I've said?" Bob broke into my thoughts.

"For one," I began slowly, "it's obvious that if I'm to lead my small church faithfully, I need to work closely with those who have the coalesced power. Up till now I've cast them in my mind as enemies, but they're really allies."

"You're a quick learner." Bob always encouraged my thoughts no matter how basic. "You'll discover that you can work effectively in any leadership situation if you understand where the leadership power resides and work with it rather than against it.

"I know it's been a long morning, and we both have to go, but let me leave you with this one last thought. Remember:

For any size church to grow, the leaders must lead.

The crucial issue is their attitude. If leaders think you can grow *or* think you can't, they're right. Their attitude becomes a type of self-fulfilling prophecy. As you have time, think about that this week."

"Will do."

Taking It Home

All week long I wrestled with the concept of coalesced leadership power. I think I know where the power resides in my church. Where do you think it resides in yours? Is it in key families, committees, elected leaders, or perhaps somewhere else? Most important, are your leaders leading? Briefly summarize your thoughts before moving on to the next part of my story.

What Is the Pastor's Role?

As I HEADED HOME from my meeting with Bob, I felt elated. When my wife saw my face, she smiled. "I can see you had another good meeting."

For the rest of the morning I related to my wife the concepts I had learned about leadership power. She listened intently, even though I am sure she was more than bored with some of the details. Later that evening I constructed mental images of various implications for my church and ministry. Turning different leadership scenarios around in my mind, my elation evaporated as I struggled to put myself into the picture. Exactly where did I fit in the leadership scheme of things? The questions kept me awake during the night as my mind played mental gymnastics with the various options.

The next day I called Bob to express my frustration. He was in a brief staff meeting, but his secretary kindly took my name and number adding a promise that Bob would call me soon. About twenty minutes later, Bob returned my call.

"After all the time we spent together over the last couple of weeks," Bob kidded, "I thought you'd be tired of talking to me."

"No, on the contrary, talking to you is a blessing," I countered. "What we explored regarding leadership was a good start," I said. "It also left me with a crucial question."

"Okay, I'll bite. What's the question that's been keeping you up all night?"

"Well," I answered, "exactly where do I fit into the leadership of my church?"

"That's a little involved. Do you have some time to talk right now?" Bob asked.

"I sure do!"

My friend continued, "I've gathered over the years that most pastors are loved by their people but they are viewed in three distinct ways."

I retrieved my notepad from a desk drawer along with the card of *McIntosh's Typology of Church Sizes.*

McIntosh's Typology of Church Sizes

Factors	Small Church	Medium Church	Large Church
Size	15–200 worshipers	201–400 worshipers	401+ worshipers
Orientation	Relational	Programmatical	Organizational
Structure	Single cell	Stretched cell	Multiple cell
Leadership	Resides in key families	Resides in committees	Resides in select leaders
Pastor	Lover	Administrator	Leader

"It won't surprise you that these three views fit reasonably well with how small, medium, and large churches see their pastor."

While Bob talked, I quickly outlined a chart and said, "Go on."

"In a small congregation people customarily see their pastor from a relational point of view. A study completed some years ago found that members of small churches used some of the following phrases to praise their pastor.[12]

- Our minister loves everyone!
- He's such a warm and kindhearted person that we all love him.
- Everyone in the community respects him.
- He's got a real sense of humor.
- The kids all like him.
- He cares for us and knows us by name.
- He treats everyone the same.

"Looking at the big picture, members of small churches stress the personal characteristics of the pastor. Some of the most commonly used words to describe the pastor in these churches are *loving, warm, caring,* and *kindhearted*."

"I have no trouble understanding this," I replied. "We already discussed that small churches are relationally oriented and it's logical that they'd want a pastor who reflects that orientation."

"Correct. As we move on to the medium-sized church, a significant change takes place in the perception of the church members."

Marveling at Bob's ability to simplify complex issues with such clarity, I said, "Keep talking. I'm writing this all down so I won't forget any of it."

"Medium-sized congregations perceive their pastor from a functional viewpoint. In the study I mentioned before, church members of medium-sized churches spoke of their pastor with some of the following statements.

- He's a great planner.
- Our pastor is an organizer.
- He's a good teacher.

61

- The pastor has put together a good administrative team.
- He's a superb preacher.
- Our pastor is one of the most creative people I've known.
- He's well prepared for every meeting.

"As you can tell, there is a subtle shift in the way people view their pastor depending on what size church they're in. Words such as *organizer, administrator, teacher,* and *supervisor* are all functional terms. Within reason, the way the pastor functions in a medium church appears to be slightly more important than his relationships."

I wrote that down and then asked, "Aren't relationships important in all churches?"

"Yes, all ministry has a fundamental relational quality about it. There is a vertical relationship with God and a horizontal one with our brothers and sisters in Christ. However, as a church grows, the manner in which people view their pastor changes slightly. The growing complexity of the medium-sized church places greater emphasis on functional skills, mirrored in the comments made by church members of medium-sized churches."

"You mean," I commented, "relational skills continue to be important to a pastor in any size church, but the changing complexity of the church creates a need for additional skills."

"That's a good summary. Perhaps it'll be even clearer after we consider larger churches. Going back to the study mentioned before, members of large churches view their pastor as a professional. They make comments such as:

- Our pastor has assembled a great staff.
- He's really got this church moving forward.
- If he'd gone into business, he'd be president of the company.
- He's an outstanding leader.
- Our pastor is a visionary.

- He's a good strategist.
- The pastor has everyone pulling together.

"These comments picture the pastor of a large church as a professional who is able to lead, dream, motivate, strategize, and coordinate a fruitful ministry. As a general rule, the larger the church, the greater the demands of the congregation that the pastor be a leader."

"Let me venture a summary," I said. "What you're saying is that as the size of a church increases, the perception of a pastor changes from an emphasis on relational skills, to functional skills, to leadership skills."

"It's more complex than that but put simply that's about it," Bob agreed.

"Okay," I pressed, "what are some ramifications of all this?"

"As you may guess, there are too many ramifications for us to discuss over the phone today. However, give me a few more minutes of your time, and I'll share the major ones with you."

I replied, "*I'm* taking *your* time. But if you have a few more minutes, as they say, I'm all ears."

"The first implication that comes to mind is that a church is most likely to attract a pastor who fits its perspective. For example, large churches tend to think in professional terms and therefore attract a pastor who is a leader. Since small churches view life relationally, they'll likely choose a pastor that supports that focus of ministry. This generally holds true with all three sizes of church.

"A second implication is if these different viewpoints are taken seriously by people and pastor, they can provide an objective evaluation for offering or accepting a call to pastor a particular church. A pastor who loves to be with people one-on-one is likely to be frustrated in a medium-sized church. A small congregation that desires a pastor who loves people will likely be unhappy with a pastor whose primary gifts are functional.

"A third major implication is that these different viewpoints explain occasional mismatches of pastor and people. When the gifts, talents, interests, experiences, and skills of a pastor match the church's needs, personality, strengths, and resources, there is potential for a good match. The better the quality of the match, the higher the potential for growth. Of course, it sometimes happens that a mismatch occurs. A few years ago, I recall a pastor who was called from Montana to serve a church in southern California. The pastor had ministered with distinction in a small congregation in Montana, seeing it grow to more than two hundred worshipers. However, after serving what was originally a five-hundred-member church in southern California for less than eighteen months, he abruptly resigned, due to staggering losses in attendance. Both the pastor and the people questioned what had gone wrong. Looking back, they realized it was a clear mismatch. Following what all viewed as a failed ministry experience, this same pastor accepted a new church in Wyoming and once again did exceptionally well.

"I should mention that mismatches often take place due to what is called the pendulum effect. Just as the pendulum swings back and forth on a clock, it's common for churches to swing back and forth in what they look for in a pastor. A small church that loses a pastor who focused on developing loving relationships may sense a need for better administration. However, after calling a new pastor with greater administrative skills, they'll soon long for a pastor with more relational skills. So the pendulum goes back and forth from one pastor to another. If they understood fully the different needs of churches, they might make a more balanced selection when calling a new pastor.

"One last implication is that to lead effectively, pastors need to adjust their ministry skills to fit the church where they serve. For example, a pastor who is highly skilled as an organizer or administrator but finds himself in a small church should modify his approach. He must temporarily minister more relationally than he normally might. Later on, after he has gained trust and after the church has grown, he can gradually shift back into his more natural leadership style. Of course the opposite is also true. A pastor with strengths in one-on-one relationships must adapt to a different style as a functional or professional leader as the church grows. This is the reason it's so uncommon for the same pastor to lead a church through all the stages of growth from small to medium to large. The adaptation of skills needed to make the transitions of leadership is more difficult than one might imagine. I've got an excellent chart that will illustrate the changes a pastor must go through regarding leadership style. I'll fax it to you when we're finished talking."

The chart below is the one Bob faxed to me later in the day. Note how the pastoral role changes as the church grows larger. When pastoring a small church with a relational orientation, a wise pastor will personally minister alongside everyone else in the church. As an example, if the small church plans a workday, the pastor will be expected to be there working with all the other members of the church. As the church grows into a middle-sized church, the pastor will need to function more like a supervisor or middle manager. Using the example of a church workday, the pastor may be there but he will focus on directing or coordinating others' work. When the church becomes a large church, the pastor's role must change to that of upper management. You will rarely see the top management of IBM cleaning the grounds around corporate headquarters. Likewise, when the large church has a workday, the members will not expect the pastor to be there.

Size	Pastoral Role
2,000+	chairman
800–1999	president
350–799	top management
250–349	middle management
200–249	supervisor
75–199	foreman
55–74	lead man
30–55	skilled worker
1–29	worker

"I don't want to take too much more of your day," I said, "but I do have many more questions regarding pastoral leadership."

"God must be in this," Bob explained. "My secretary just handed me a note saying my ten o'clock appointment is canceled. So, I've got another thirty minutes to talk."

"Great! Considering our conversation yesterday on leadership power, does it ever coalesce in the senior pastor? I've observed that some pastors seem to have no problem in casting a vision, motivating people to follow, and providing, as you said, the oomph to get it done. I just don't understand how it comes about. I think it would take years for me to establish that level of leadership."

"You're right again! It does take years for leadership power to coalesce in the pastor. The central issue has to do with continuity."

"What do you mean by continuity?" I asked.

"In every church, people place their trust in what is constant. In the small church the constant factor that provides ongoing continuity year after year is the key family or long-term leaders. Members of the church realize that pastors come and go, and along with them come and go different approaches to ministry. This is why key families have so much leadership power in a small church. Say a new pastor is called to a small church. He will normally seek to establish a new direction complete with new programs, but the members look to the long-term leaders for approval. Why? Because they've seen other pastors come in with their so-called bag of tricks and then leave. The key families will always be there; they have the leadership power in that situation.

"Now as the church grows into a medium-sized church, the programs begin to provide the continuity. For instance, in many medium churches today, a private Christian school is a central and powerful ministry. Leaders may come and go, but the Christian school will remain a constant force providing continuity to the overall ministry. Other ministries provide similar continuity, such as a youth program, children's program, Sunday school, or missions program. As we discussed before, the leadership power coalesces in the committees and leaders who oversee these programs. If you ever doubt the truth of this, just try to fire a beloved principal or youth pastor.

"To finally get to your question, in the large church the continuity often is the senior pastor or in some situations a staff member. You've no doubt read that growing churches normally have pastors with a long tenure. Research has discovered that long pastoral tenures don't guarantee a church will grow. However, short pastoral tenures almost always guarantee a church will not grow. The reason is this issue of continuity. The longer a pastor's tenure, the more he provides the continuity for the church and the more likely leadership power will coalesce in him."

"This makes sense, but I'm concerned that many pastors today just seem to be glorified CEOs. I don't think it's a very biblical concept. It seems like just another example of how the business world has invaded the church."

"I'm aware of what you're saying. Personally I believe that people in our churches can spot a glory hog or ego tripper or ladder climber a mile away. If by CEO you mean that type of leader, I don't think we have much to fear. In most situations church members won't lay down their life for a senior pastor's ego or blind ambition; although, I must admit it has happened in a few cases.

"The real issue is leadership, and one doesn't have to act like a corporate CEO to be a leader. The Greek word for leadership is *proistemi,* which means 'to stand before.' This same word is translated 'to manage,' as in one's family (1 Tim. 3:4); 'to direct,' as in the affairs of the church (1 Tim. 5:17); and 'to rule,' as in governing (Rom. 12:8). Thus the central idea of a leader is standing before people and leading them in some direction. Many people, of course, stand before the congregation as leaders. But the pastor is the person up front and out front most often, which is the essence of leadership. Some people object to the pastor being the leader of the church, but that's the role God has given him.

"Since the early 1970s a large number of studies have been conducted on growing churches in North America. A persistent thread running through all this research has been the need for a high caliber of pastoral leadership. Second only to the empowering work of the Holy Spirit, pastoral leadership is the most determinative factor in growing churches. Any church that desires to develop a healthy ministry must adequately recognize that strong pastoral competence is a decisive factor for the vitality and outreach of their congregation."

"I've got to do some more thinking about pastoral leadership," I admitted.

"Studying leadership is a lifelong journey," Bob commented. "Discussion on what makes a leader and what constitutes leadership will certainly continue into the future. Over the last twenty-nine years of ministry, I've made seven discoveries about pastoral leadership in the church. Let me give you a brief synopsis and we can talk about them later.

"First, I've discovered that the best teams have great leaders. A popular trend in the church today is the use of teams. Team ministry is clearly a biblical approach. Christ modeled it with his twelve disciples, the early church selected a team of deacons, and Paul appointed elders in churches. Teams do a good job of discussing ideas, debating issues, and setting policy. The truth is, however, they provide little leadership. Teams without a good leader tend to flounder.

"Second, the leader's task is to cast a vision. I like to view a church as a house. The main floor is where most of the day-to-day work of ministry is done. The second floor is where the plans for ministry are designed. The top is where the vision (or dream) for ministry is formed. The main job of a leader is to live in the top of the house forming and communicating God's vision and values to the congregation. In most cases this person must be the senior pastor because no one else has the overall perspective or opportunity to communicate to the entire congregation.

"Third, God reveals his vision to one person. It has been my observation from the Bible and in personal ministry that teams do not develop vision. God delights to give his vision for ministry to a single individual who then shares it with the team. Of course, the team helps shape the vision by asking questions and clarifying certain issues, but the initiation of the vision comes from a single person.

"Fourth, leadership authority grows over time. John Maxwell, a popular lecturer on leadership, illustrates this truth through what he calls five levels of leadership. A person begins leading from a position of rights (level 1). As time goes by, leadership authority grows as strong relationships are developed (level 2). The ministry then demonstrates good results (level 3), leaders are reproduced (level 4), and people develop respect for the leader (level 5). To progress from level one to level five may take fifteen to twenty years in some situations.[13] That's why I always say,

Leadership authority must be earned through faithful service.

To demand leadership authority is to lose it before you get it.

"Fifth, leadership authority may be lost in a moment. The one thing that scares me the most about leadership authority is not how long it takes to develop, but how quickly it may be lost. What may take twenty years to develop may be lost in a moment. There are certain things a leader simply cannot get away with, such as involvement in immoral activities and unethical behavior. Leaders must guard their spiritual life daily.

"Sixth, if you don't lead, someone else will. An observant person once noted that leadership abhors a vacuum. On any team, board, committee, or group, if a leadership void exists, someone will eventually move into the position of leader. If God called you to be the pastor of a church, he has called you to set the agenda for its future. I can guarantee you that if you're not the leader, someone else will be. And, many times it's someone you'd rather not have lead.

"And, seventh, the law of the whale is always at work."

Barely containing myself, I burst out, "What? What's the law of the whale?"

I could almost see Bob smiling as he continued, "The law of the whale declares,

Whenever you rise to the surface and blow, you'll get harpooned.

Others have said it differently. For instance, a wise friend of mine told me once in my first church, 'The tallest tree catches the most wind.' Or as a Persian proverb says, 'The larger a man's roof, the more snow it collects.' Since effective leaders promote new ideas and set direction, they become criticism collectors. If you aren't receiving any criticism, don't jump to the conclusion that you're doing a great job and pleasing everyone. The lack of criticism may merely mean you have put up a small roof. If you choose to be a leader by setting a new direction for your people, you'll be criticized. It simply comes with the territory. But . . . you'll be in good company."

Here is my summary of Bob's theories on pastoral leadership:

1. Teams need a good leader or they will flounder.
2. The leader's task is to cast a vision.

3. God reveals his vision to one person.
4. Leadership authority in the church grows over time.
5. Leadership authority may be lost in a moment.
6. If the pastor doesn't lead, someone else will.
7. Leaders attract criticism.

Taking It Home

When Bob faxed over his chart illustrating the transitions of pastoral leadership in a growing church, he included the following principles that I thought you would enjoy seeing. I have labeled them "Bob's Advice for Leadership."

1. **Love the Lord.** How are you showing God you love him in your life and ministry?
2. **Grow the people.** What process do you have in place to disciple the people in your church?
3. **Dream a big dream.** What passion do you have for the future development of your church?
4. **Lead by example.** How are you modeling God's truth to your family and ministry team?
5. **Take initiative.** Are you taking steps of faith to accomplish God's vision for your church?
6. **Take risks.** Are you willing to struggle and fail sometimes before you see signs of growth?
7. **Trust in the Lord.** Are you planting and watering, trusting God to bring in the harvest?

In which of these seven principles are you the strongest? Which one represents your greatest weakness?

6

How Are Decisions Made?

I APPRECIATED BOB'S TAKING TIME from his busy schedule to talk to me on the phone. Before our conversation ended, Bob
asked if I could come to his office at church for lunch next time,
rather than meet for breakfast. I gladly agreed. Actually I had
wanted to see my friend's church facility for a long time, and this
provided the opportunity.

When I arrived at Bob's church, his secretary showed me into
his office, and Bob got up from his desk to shake my hand. "I hope
you like pepperoni pizza," he said. "I took the liberty of ordering
lunch so we could talk right here."

"It's my favorite," I replied.

Bob got right to the point. "I have only ninety minutes for lunch
today, so let's move into our next topic. Did you bring along the
card of *McIntosh's Typology of Church Sizes?*"

"Yes, I've got it right here." I pulled it out of my briefcase and handed it to Bob.

He glanced at the card and said, "The next subject we need to discuss is how decisions are made in small, medium, and large churches."

Peeking at the card, I noticed it read:

McIntosh's Typology of Church Sizes

Factors	Small Church	Medium Church	Large Church
Size	15–200 worshipers	201–400 worshipers	401+ worshipers
Orientation	Relational	Programmatical	Organizational
Structure	Single cell	Stretched cell	Multiple cell
Leadership	Resides in key families	Resides in committees	Resides in select leaders
Pastor	Lover	Administrator	Leader
Decisions	Made by congregation	Made by committees	Made by staff and leaders
	Driven by history	Driven by changing needs	Driven by vision

Knowing that we had a limited amount of time, Bob launched into his discussion of how decisions are made in different size churches.

"Pastors and other leaders are called on to make many important decisions that affect the future of a church's ministry in its community. Decision making is not accomplished in a void. On the contrary, each size church usually operates out of a particular frame of reference. This frame of reference creates an unseen decision-making grid through which various decisions are sifted before being finalized. The church's personality, purpose, values, goals, traditions, customs, and expectations represent some, but not all, of the decision-making grid.

"History reveals that in most small churches, *decisions are made by the congregation* with heavy influence from a single person, family, or families. It is quite common in small churches for the real decisions to be made informally in the parking lot or around the kitchen table in someone's home before any formal decision is determined. In these churches tradition and custom often drive the decision-making process. Direction by the pastor is far less influential. Thus it is normal in a great number of small churches for the decision-making grid to include concerns such as keeping people happy, meeting the budget, reducing use of the building, re-creating yesterday, keeping expenditures as low as possible, maintaining the status quo of relationships, and minimizing dissent."

"That has been my experience in this church," I agreed. "While I've challenged the people to a greater vision, every decision for the past six months has favored the inward concerns you've mentioned."

"Uh-huh! That's predictable. Now when we think about how decisions occur in a medium-sized church, it's quite different. For example, since a medium-sized church is going through a transitional phase, decisions about adding volunteers, hiring more staff, dealing with increased complexity, motivating stewardship, co-ordinating facility usage, or establishing policies are often *driven by changing needs.* Since the leadership power resides in boards and committees, that is where new ministry ideas originate, and the major decisions are hammered out and agreed on before they even go to the congregation for confirmation.

"As a case in point, when this church was growing through the middle-sized phase, we started receiving lots of requests from people outside the church to use our building for weddings. We'd never received such requests when the church was smaller because the sanctuary didn't appeal to people. When the church grew, we remodeled the sanctuary. The word got around that the sanctuary was beautiful, and people began to call. We decided it would be best to define a wedding policy and it was worked out by a special task force. After the task force drafted a wedding policy, they gave it to every church committee for review. After all the committees had commented on the policy, the task force wrote a final draft, which was brought to the governing board. The board passed it and presented it to the congregation. Not a single person dissented since it had been developed at the correct level by the right people."

"I can see how that fit in with the orientation of a midsize church," I commented. Actually Bob was talking so fast I could barely take notes, let alone try to add anything to the conversation.

"Now, when we look at how large churches make decisions, the process changes once again. The general rule is that the larger church expects the senior pastor to be the initiating leader. In most situations this translates into *the senior pastor and his staff being the primary decision makers along with the main governing board* of lay leaders. Quite often the governing board of the large church acts as a policy-setting group and delegates to the pastor and staff the everyday decisions on running the church. If the leadership power resides in the senior pastor, it is easy to see how influential he will be in the decision-making process. For the most part, in decisions they make, large churches depend quite heavily on the pastor's vision of the future."

"The pizza's here." Bob's secretary carried in a large pizza box and two soft drinks.

Trying to hold my slice of pizza on a napkin, take notes, and talk nearly overpowered my dexterity, but somehow I managed to ask, "It's obvious how a pastor in a larger church influences the decision making, but how does someone like me, the pastor of a smaller church, influence the decision-making process? Or for that matter, how does a pastor in a middle-sized church get things accomplished in a committee environment?"

"In small churches the dominant control over decision making appears to be in the hands of the key family or families, the finance committee, and then the pastor. Pastors who successfully lead small churches take initiative and influence the decision-making process through relationships. Let me give you an example. A friend of mine pastored a church averaging around one hundred in worship in a facility that sat on one and a half acres of land. Bordering the church property were an additional two acres of vacant land. God gave my friend the vision to purchase that extra piece of property. He knew that the additional property would allow the church to expand its parking as well as provide greater visibility, which would aid in the growth of the church. In a larger church a pastor might just announce that God had given him a vision to buy the property, but he knew such an approach wouldn't work in a small church."

"Okay, I can see how that fits," I nodded. "So . . . what did he do?"

"My friend decided to share his vision with the deacons of his church one by one. He arranged to take each deacon to lunch individually. Each time, he asked a deacon to meet him at the church, and they took one car to a local restaurant. When they returned to the church parking lot and got out of the car, the pastor would draw the deacon's attention to the vacant lot next door and ask, 'Do you think God would ever allow us to buy that property?' Using this question as a starting point, the two of them would enter into a discussion of the needs and benefits of obtaining the property.

"My friend worked his way through each deacon and other informal leaders in the church. Each time he followed the same steps. The interesting thing is he never mentioned the possibility of buying the property in a sermon, board meeting, or business meeting. However, after about eight months of talking with leaders one by one, at one board meeting one of the board members said, 'I've been thinking a lot lately about that vacant property next door. I think we should buy it before someone else beats us to it.' Before long, the church had entered into escrow for the property."

Taking advantage of an opportunity to speak, I asked, "Isn't that manipulative?"

"No!" Bob shot back. "It's leadership!"

"Leadership?"

"Leadership! Think back to what we've been discussing. You don't lead small churches by telling them what to do. You lead small churches by establishing a relationship of trust with the key people and then helping them discover needs and opportunities. If you can lovingly assist them to see the issues, they'll eventually make the decisions to move forward. Manipulation happens only when people no longer have a choice. My pastor friend didn't remove his people's choice by undue pressure. Instead, he helped them see the opportunities and left the choice to them. That's leadership!"

"And in the medium church?" I inquired.

"In the medium church a pastor must meet with each committee, task force, team, or board. Instead of meeting with each individual deacon, like my friend did, the pastor would meet with each committee or board chairperson. It's best if an idea can be initiated at the committee level by a respected person other than the pastor. Influencing the decision-making process in this way is not politicking it's …"

"I know. I know. It's leadership."

"You got it!"

"While we're on this subject of decision making, I've noticed that small churches become emotional over decisions. A number of years ago, I was in a small church that needed to replace the linoleum in the church kitchen. It was incredible how emotional everyone became when they tried to decide on color. I thought the decision was going to cause a church split!"

"You're describing what is called decision-making climate. Let me draw you another picture."

Bob stood up and moved to a white board that hung on a wall in his office. Taking a marker, he drew the continuum below.

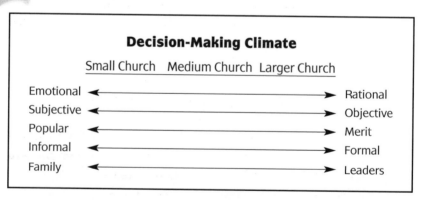

Decision-Making Climate

Small Church   Medium Church Larger Church

Emotional	⟵————————⟶	Rational
Subjective	⟵————————⟶	Objective
Popular	⟵————————⟶	Merit
Informal	⟵————————⟶	Formal
Family	⟵————————⟶	Leaders

"The continuum I've drawn moves from the small church, through the medium church, to the large church, and back. You can see how the decision-making climate changes as we move along the continuum. The smaller the church the more likely the decision will be emotional and subjective. Choices are determined on the basis of the speaker's popularity and ties to the main families in the church. It's not uncommon for decisions to be made rather informally by key people as they play golf, eat dinner, or talk in the parking lot before church.

"The larger the church becomes, the more the probability increases that judgments will be made rationally and objectively. Whether or not an issue has merit becomes the deciding factor rather than the popularity of the speaker. Choices are made formally and with more direction by selected leaders.

"Medium churches reflect a little of each side of the continuums depending on how much they reflect a small church or large church ideology. Part of the awkwardness of medium-sized churches is due to the reality that they can reverberate back and forth on the continuums, sometimes making decisions rationally and the next time more emotionally."

"That's helpful in knowing how the process works in various size churches, but do you have any guidelines that might assist me and my leaders in our decision-making responsibilities?"

"I sure do," smiled my mentor. He handed me a small card with the heading "Five Guiding Principles of Effective Ministry."

Bob continued, "It's wise to run every decision through this grid. The first principle is that of *visionary leadership.* Jesus came to seek and save the lost. His last words to his disciples, which we call the Great Commission, summarized his entire ministry. I realize you know this passage, but it's good for us to read it fresh from time to time: '. . . All authority has been given to Me in heaven and on earth. Go therefore and make disciples of all the nations, baptizing them in the name of the Father and the Son and the Holy Spirit, teaching them to observe all that I commanded you; and lo, I am with you always, even to the end of the age' (Matt. 28:18–20).

"Churches that make decisions based only on how this will affect their current members or worshipers are generally not growing churches. We must ask, Will this decision increase our church's effectiveness at winning people to Jesus Christ?"

"That's a question I wish my church would take seriously," I said. "What about the next principle?"

79

Five Guiding Principles of Effective Ministry

1. **The Principle of Visionary Leadership**
   A church grows when decisions are made based on the intention of bringing new people into the church.

2. **The Principle of Human Resource Utilization**
   A church grows when decisions provide the staff, leadership, and resources needed to focus on outreach.

3. **The Principle of "Open Doors"**
   A church grows when decisions create opportunities for new people to enter into the life of the congregation.

4. **The Principle of Incorporation**
   A church grows when decisions spawn ways to incorporate new people into the social circles of the membership.

5. **The Principle of Finance**
   A church grows when decisions adequately finance local outreach activities.

"The second guiding principle for decision making focuses on the *utilization of human resources*. I think every church needs an HR department. The way churches use the human resources God has given them is crucial to the development of the church internally and externally. Studies have determined that there should be one full-time pastoral staff person for every 150 worshipers. This allows adequate professional resources to maintain and expand the ministry. Observation also shows that when 60 percent of the worshipers of a church have a ministry in the church, it aids the growth of the church. A minimum of 10 percent of those serving in the church must be involved in outreach. So churches must ask, Will this decision effectively utilize our professional and volunteer staff both for maintaining and expanding our ministry?"

"What a novel idea! Establishing a human resource department in a church for lay ministry could be a great way to put into practice the priesthood of all believers. Keep going. These are good questions."

"Are there open doors for new people? This question is a way to frame the third principle of *open doors*. We know it would be very difficult to enter a house without doors. What church leaders may not recognize is that church doors are not always open. Open doors allow newcomers an opportunity to enter into the life and ministry of a church. Closed doors or doors that don't exist keep newcomers out. Doors can be anything from the worship service to a divorce recovery group or an athletic program. Church leaders must constantly seek to create new doors so that new people are able to enter the life of their church. Thus growing churches ask, Will this decision create new opportunities for new people to enter the life of our congregation?"

"There are very few doors through which new people may enter into my church," I observed. "My leaders need to ask and answer this question for themselves as soon as possible."

Bob went on. "The fourth principle of *incorporation* addresses the need to welcome or assimilate new people into the social networks of a church. The dynamics of inclusion in and exclusion from groups are real and significant. These dynamics are at work every day in all our lives, whether it is on a girls' softball team, a women's sewing group, or a Sunday school class. Newcomers don't stay long if they feel like outsiders. The feeling of being wanted, having a sense of identity, and belonging to a group are strong pulls for a newcomer's personal involvement. A church should be a place where new people can find acceptance in Christ and fellowship with his people. Unfortunately many churches shut out new people without realizing it. Effective churches always ask, Will this decision exclude newcomers or help include them in the life of our church?

"Finally there is the principle of *finance*. Just about any human endeavor takes a financial investment. Growing churches spend from 5 to 10 percent of their total budget for outreach in their local ministry areas. While money alone doesn't assure growth, without financial resources directed toward outreach, growth seldom occurs. If our personal checkbook reveals where our heart is, how much more does the church's checkbook reveal where its heart is? The last question a church needs to ask is, Will this decision allow for adequate financing of our local outreach activities?"[14]

"These principles certainly hit home with me," I said. "I'll share them with my leaders, one by one of course, and see if we can use them as a grid for future decisions."

"Your next appointment is due in ten minutes, Pastor." Bob's secretary was great at keeping him on schedule.

"Ninety minutes goes fast when you're having fun. Thanks for coming to my office today," Bob said as he stood to walk me to the door. "Say, would you like a tour of the facility?"

"I sure would," I said.

"I'll see if we can find someone to show you around."

"Thanks!"

Taking It Home

Bob's Five Guiding Principles of Effective Ministry really hit home with me. Over the following weeks I met with each of my board members and discussed these principles. Later at one of our board meetings we evaluated our decision-making process to see how each of these questions could be used creatively. Think back to the last few decisions made in your church. Then evaluate how the decisions might have been different if you had asked each of the following five key questions.

1. Will this decision increase our church's effectiveness at winning people to Jesus Christ?

_____

_____

_____

2. Will this decision effectively utilize our professional and volunteer staff both for maintaining and expanding our ministry?

_____

_____

_____

3. Will this decision create new opportunities for new people to enter the life of our congregation?

_____

_____

_____

4. Will this decision exclude newcomers or help include them in the life of our church?

_____

_____

_____

5. Will this decision allow for adequate financing of our local outreach activities?

_____

_____

_____

7

What Is the Impact of Staff?

DURING THE WEEKS AFTER Bob and I first began to meet, I started incorporating much of what I had learned into my ministry. I even made changes in the way I approached my leaders. For example, in place of challenging my board as a group to think about the future, I focused on each board member individually. I took each of my board members out for breakfast or lunch to become better acquainted. During our first meeting, I asked each leader individually to share his personal story of faith, as well as how he had come to our church. The second time we met I asked each one to tell me what he saw in the future for our church. After listening to their hopes for our church, I then offered to share some of my thoughts. Each one said he would like to know what future I saw for the church. It is funny, though we never actually used the word *vision,* that is what we were formulating as we told our stories, hopes, and dreams for the future.

What was eye-opening, however, was the response of the board members. After meeting with each person twice, I could tell that each one looked at me differently. Tension melted away and I felt they respected me more. Of course, this was just the beginning. I had a long way to go to earn leadership authority, but it was a good start.

Putting into practice a relational leadership style took patience and practice on my part. I am thankful that the people gave me time to grow and develop. However, old frustrations kept resurfacing. Since I had previously ministered in multiple staff settings, I was challenged by being the only pastor. It seemed like the people expected me to do everything. In addition to my normal pastoral duties, I selected the songs, wrote out the order of worship, typed the Sunday bulletin, printed it, and even folded it. Previous pastors were responsible for cleaning the church building and mowing the lawn around the church facility and parsonage. This was a totally new concept to me, one with which I was not entirely happy.

I can still remember the confrontation one trustee and I had shortly after I was installed as the new pastor. The grass around the church was growing quite long and I asked when the trustees were going to mow the lawn. To my surprise the trustee informed me, "The previous pastor always mowed the lawn."

"Well," I shot back, "I'll mow the lawn around the parsonage, since that's my home, but the lawn around the church is up to the trustees." I'm sure that little exchange did not help our relationship any. Although I believe it was proper to keep that "monkey" off my back, I could have handled it in a friendlier manner.

For me, a question still lingered: How does the issue of staff fit with small, medium, and large churches? I knew some of the answers but felt that Bob could shed more light on the subject. So I phoned him again.

"You've hit on another dominant difference between small, medium, and large churches," he responded. "The number of staff and the way they are organized impacts churches for growth and decline." Bob did not have time to talk by phone and suggested we discuss the topic of staff at our breakfast meeting the following day.

The next day we met for breakfast at our usual place. As we sat down, Bob began, "So you are struggling with the contrasts of single staff and multiple staff."

"Yes," I said, "like I told you yesterday when I phoned, my past experience has always been in larger churches with multiple staffs. Being the lone pastor is a new experience. What are the different dynamics of a single pastor versus multiple staff?"

"It's my belief that God intended ministry to be a team approach," my mentor said. "It's clear that Jesus formed a team with his twelve disciples, and so did Paul and Barnabas as we see in the Book of Acts. Growth leadership in each size church must be orchestrated through a team. My favorite analogy of the differences in staffing between small, medium, and large churches is attributed to my friend and noted expert on large churches, Dr. John Vaughn.[15]

The leadership team in a small church is like a duet. The leadership team in a medium-sized church is like a quartet. The leadership team in a large church is like an ensemble.

87

"In the small, solo pastor church the leadership team is like a *duet—pastor and people.* The staffing dynamic is fairly simple as only two parties are involved. Planning takes place informally. A direct line to the pastor is available to all church members, which smooths the communication process. As long as the members of the duet do their part, the potential for harmony is high. This duet continues to be the best understood form of staffing a church and the one in which many people feel most comfortable."

"That makes sense," I suggested, "since most churches are small."

"As the church grows into a medium-sized church," Bob continued, "the leadership team becomes *a complex quartet composed of pastor, a small staff, lay leaders, and the congregation.* Communication dynamics increase sixfold, making the medium church a high risk stage in staff development. Since more parties are involved, there is a greater chance that one member of the team will not carry through his or her responsibilities, causing the rest of the team and the church to suffer.

"In the large church the leadership team becomes *an ensemble with pastor, a large multiple staff, numerous lay leaders, multiple secretaries and support personnel, and the congregation.* Instructions and assignments are made formally and in writing since task assignments cannot be taken for granted. The senior pastor must increasingly function like the leader of a choir composed of sections and coordinated by section leaders. Pastors who are unable to delegate management of secondary level staff members to an associate usually become preoccupied with maintenance and retard their edge as growth leaders.

"Look at the card with the McIntosh typologies," Bob said.

I took it out and glanced at the row labeled "Staff."

"It sounds like you've had experience with each one of these sizes," I said.

"That's right," Bob agreed. "Each size has its challenges. But the crucial question is, Is the church staffed to decline, remain on a plateau, or grow? To answer this question, let's start with the small church once again and work our way through the three sizes."

McIntosh's Typology of Church Sizes

Factors	Small Church	Medium Church	Large Church
Size	15–200 worshipers	201–400 worshipers	401+ worshipers
Orientation	Relational	Programmatical	Organizational
Structure	Single cell	Stretched cell	Multiple cell
Leadership	Resides in key families	Resides in committees	Resides in select leaders
Pastor	Lover	Administrator	Leader
Decisions	Made by congregation Driven by history	Made by committees Driven by changing needs	Made by staff and leaders Driven by vision
Staff	Bivocational or single pastor	Pastor and small staff	Multiple staff

"Okay."

"Small churches are normally pastored by a bivocational or single pastor. Once upon a time, the vast majority of churches were pastored by what today we call bivocational pastors. This approach to staffing a church is modeled after the apostle Paul in Acts 18:3 where he worked as a tentmaker to provide his own financial support for the ministry. It's likely that Peter, Andrew, James, and John used this model and earned their living as fishermen. Basically a tentmaker or bivocational pastor is one who derives the majority of his financial support from outside the local church. In the United States this model continued to be a norm into and slightly beyond the westward frontier movement. With the growth of seminaries and a more professional pastorate, the use of bivocational ministers declined some but has never been totally abandoned."

"Are there many bivocational pastors today?" I asked.

"Yes, many church leaders believe there is a revival of tentmaking pastors today and they predict this trend will increase in the next decade. Already substantial percentages of tentmakers are found ministering in the Episcopal Church, Presbyterian Church (USA), American Baptist Churches/USA, several black denominations, the Southern Baptist Convention, Pentecostal, independent church groups, and others."

"I'd assume a bivocational pastor faces issues that even I don't see," I commented.

"That's correct. The basic challenges facing bivocational pastors are those of balancing two work positions and managing work, church, and family responsibilities. Bivocational ministry usually doesn't work well when both the secular and church positions are time-consuming. It appears that the most difficult aspect of bivocational ministry is keeping limits clear so as not to end up with two full-time jobs."

"Fortunately I'm in a church that pays almost a full-time salary," I noted, "even though I work a few hours a week as a salesman to make some extra money."

"I'd call you a moonlighter," Bob suggested. "Bivocational pastors make most of their income from a job other than the pastorate. You wouldn't be classified a bivocational pastor since you make most of your income from your church ministry."

"I see."

"Actually about 70 percent of those in bivocational ministry choose that type of ministry, believing it is beneficial. For instance, working bivocationally helps pastors stay attuned to the tensions, struggles, and needs of the working church member.[16] A recent study by the Southern Baptist Sunday School Board is interesting. It indicates that bivocational pastors are as effective as full-time pastors in most of their churches."[17]

"I don't sense a call to bivocational ministry but I can see that such a ministry can be useful," I said.

"Yes, bivocational ministry is an effective way for very small, financially strapped, and geographically isolated churches to carry on their mission. However, most researchers admit that it's extremely rare to see a bivocational church growing. If, as I suggested before, our mission is to fulfill our Lord's Great Commission to make disciples, then an adequate staff is crucial. A church with a bivocational pastor is at best staffed for plateau.

"The first step toward an adequate staff begins when a small church obtains the services of a full-time pastor. During the 1950s and '60s it was generally assumed that twelve tithing families could support a full-time pastor. I doubt that this was ever completely accurate, but several factors during those years made it more likely that a small church could afford a full-time pastor. Cash salaries and benefit packages for pastors were lower; there was less competition for church members' charitable contributions, so members contributed a higher portion of their income to their church; the generation that was in leadership accepted financial sacrifice due to the experience of the Great Depression and World War II; land and facility costs were fairly reasonable; and there were lower expectations concerning programs in the church.

"Of course, this has all changed during the past half century. Pastoral salaries have increased and the rise in health care insurance costs have driven benefit packages higher; church members now demand a greater variety and higher quality of church programming; costs for purchasing land and building facilities have skyrocketed into the millions; numerous charitable organizations and causes now vie for church members' dollars; and the generation now leading churches has experienced a strong economy and isn't comfortable with financial sacrifice.

"These and other changes mean it now takes about 150 adult worshipers to provide for a full-time pastor *and* to finance a church ministry that meets the expectations of today's churchgoers."

"That explains why I need to work as a part-time salesperson a few nights a week to make ends meet," I added.

"That's right," Bob agreed. "While there are always some smaller churches that can afford a full-time pastor and provide an adequate ministry, it's getting harder for many to do so. Thus one of the chal-

91

lenges for the small church is to reach the point where it can provide for a full-time pastor. Look at this chart comparing church size and staff models.

Church	Size	Staff Model
Large	401+	**Ensemble Model** • multiple staff
Medium	201–400	**Quartet Model** • pastor and small staff
Small	1–200 76–200 1–75	**Duet Model** • single pastor • bivocational pastor

"While there are exceptions, a church will find it difficult to grow beyond 75 without a full-time pastor. Once a church is able to provide for a full-time pastor, the church will then be freed to grow to between 150 and 200 people."

"I've heard of the 200 barrier," I commented. "Does staffing have anything to do with plateauing at that level?"

"Yes, it does," Bob answered. "We'll talk about the different barriers each size of church faces later, but one of the reasons a church stays smaller than 200 in worship attendance is related to the quantity of church staff. Most pastors can lead and care for 150–200 people adequately. However, the level of care and innovative leadership levels off significantly as the church approaches 200. That's when a church needs to transition into a quartet model of staffing."

"Don't some churches grow larger than 200 with only one pastor?" I quizzed.

"Certainly!" Bob granted. "I've observed, however, that in those situations, either the pastor is a workaholic or he has a super secretary who carries much of the load. In either case the church rarely grows larger than 300 worshipers before it plateaus."

"Based on your chart, it's obvious that a church needs to add another pastoral staff person when the church size reaches 200. Correct?" I asked.

"Actually not. If at all possible, a church should add a second staff person before it reaches 200 worshipers. This is how it actually works," Bob grabbed a piece of paper as he talked.

"Based on the idea that it takes 150 adults to support one pastor in a church, we can project the number of pastors needed like this." He wrote two columns of numbers on the paper.

Church Size	Pastors Needed
1–150	1
151–300	2
301–450	3
451–600	4
601–750	5
751–900	6
901–1050	7
etc.	

"Looking at this chart," Bob continued, "one might assume that a church should add a second staff person when worship attendance averages 300. Yet the church will likely never reach 300 without the second staff person. In truth it is the addition of the second staff person before or just as the church reaches 200 that enables the church to grow to 300. Then the addition of a third staff person enables the church to grow to 450 and so on."

"But isn't it financially difficult for a smaller church to add a second pastor?" I countered.

"Yes it is, and that's one reason churches don't grow larger than 200. As a church grows into the medium size of 200–400 worshipers, it must add a second and third pastor but often finds it financially difficult to pull it off. It's an awkward situation. Yet a church cannot be considered a medium-sized church until it has two or three pastors. This is one of the reasons I refer to churches under two hundred in size as small churches."

"Okay," I summarized, "for a church to grow, it must constantly monitor the total number of staff compared to its size, and then add new staff in anticipation of future growth."

"You've got it!" Bob exclaimed. "For a church to make the transition from a medium church to a large church, it will normally take a staff of four or five pastors plus additional support staff. Be aware, though, that moving from a small staff of three pastors to a multiple staff of four pastors is a difficult transition. In fact this is one of the barriers to moving past four hundred worshipers."

"What do you mean?" I asked.

"I've observed," Bob shared, "that the most difficult staff transition is from three staff members to four. I liken it to a family. When my wife and I had our first child, it seemed easy to work together as a family of three—father, mother, child. When we added a second child, we discovered the dynamics of the family changed almost 100 percent. The basic problem was that the second child always felt left out. No matter how much we tried to include her, she found it difficult to get a word in edgewise among the threesome that was already well established. Adding our third child was not nearly as difficult since the second and third child built a relationship, which allowed them to form their own small group. In a similar manner a pastoral staff of three normally works quite well, but the addition of a fourth pastor creates unexpected dynamics. I believe this is one reason churches plateau around four hundred in size. The fourth pastor often feels left out of the original pastoral threesome. When a fifth pastor is added, it provides the fourth pastor an ally. It's difficult to add that fourth staff person, which is why I often suggest a church move from three staff pastors directly to five. It just seems like it works better."

"This is fascinating," I commented, "but why don't churches invest in additional staff? It doesn't seem like this concept is too difficult to understand and apply."

"The root problem is in the priorities of a church," Bob suggested. "Many churches place their priorities in this order: facilities, programs, staff. However, you'll discover that churches with this priority list are often the declining or plateaued ones. On the other hand, churches that place their priorities in the order of staff, programs, facilities are usually the growing ones."

"That's a great insight. As my church grows in the coming years, I'll try to put those priorities into the right order."

"One last thing," Bob added as we walked to our cars. "There is no guarantee that adding staff will produce church growth, but it is rare to find a rapidly growing church that is understaffed."

"I'll remember that," I promised. "See you in a week."

Taking It Home

During the week, as I considered Bob's ideas on staffing a church, I mentally reviewed the staff situation in some of the churches I had served in over the years. In each case Bob's analysis fit well with the actual church size and number of staff. Based on Bob's teaching, how many staff members does your church need to move to the next size? What are some of the roadblocks to adding another staff person? What steps could you begin to take today to move in the right direction?

How Does Change Take Place?

Beep! Beep! Beep! Beep!

I rolled over and fumbled for the alarm clock shut off. "It can't be time to get up," I mumbled and dozed off for just a few more minutes. When finally I opened my eyes and looked at the time, I was instantly wide awake.

"It's ten after seven!" I shouted. "I'll be late for my breakfast with Bob."

By the time I showered, dressed, and drove to the restaurant, I was fifteen minutes late. "I need to buy a cell phone," I said to myself as I rushed into the restaurant.

"Coffee . . . coffee . . . I need coffee," I muttered as I approached the booth where Bob was seated.

"It looks like your day is not off to a good start!" Bob laughed as I sat down.

"Well, not exactly," I offered. "Just running a little late."

"It's okay," Bob assured me. "It gave me some time to do a little reading."

We ordered breakfast and then Bob asked, "How is your relationship with the church board developing?"

"From my viewpoint, it's going well. I sense that my board members respect me and realize now that I care for them and their church. I must admit that what we've been discussing has been a great help in turning around my relationship with them."

"That's good to hear," Bob said.

McIntosh's Typology of Church Sizes

Factors	Small Church	Medium Church	Large Church
Size	15–200 worshipers	201–400 worshipers	401+ worshipers
Orientation	Relational	Programmatical	Organizational
Structure	Single cell	Stretched cell	Multiple cell
Leadership	Resides in key families	Resides in committees	Resides in select leaders
Pastor	Lover	Administrator	Leader
Decisions	Made by congregation	Made by committees	Made by staff and leaders
	Driven by history changing needs	Driven by	Driven by vision
Staff	Bivocational or single pastor	Pastor and small staff	Multiple staff
Change	Bottom up through key people	Middle out through key committees	Top down through key leaders

"The church does need to change in some areas, however, and I'm not exactly sure how to initiate the changes."

"That's our topic for discussion today," Bob said. "Look at your copy of *McIntosh's Typology of Church Sizes.*"

"Bottom up, middle out, top down," I read. "Let me see if I can fill in the blanks."

"Okay," Bob agreed.

"Comparing this row with those above it, I'd say that the process of change in the small church is launched from the key family or other lay leaders. The pastor can be the initiator of the change, but it must be launched by the key lay leaders for ownership to be developed in the congregation."

"You're learning," Bob praised. "Let me draw you another of my famous diagrams," he joked. Bob then drew the following:

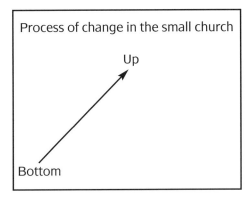

"As you've correctly noted," Bob said, "whenever change takes place in a small church, it generally takes place as the lay leaders sense a need and take the necessary steps to implement changes. Remember the story of my friend who wanted to buy the property next to his church?" Bob asked.

"Yes," I replied. "As I recall, he initiated conversation about possible changes with his board members and then waited until they implemented the steps to purchase it."

"Right! That's a good example of how change occurs from the *bottom up.* Go on," Bob encouraged.

"*Middle out* means that change in a medium church is launched through key committees, boards, or teams of people," I concluded.

"Correct again. You diagram it this time."

I took the paper from Bob and drew this illustration of the concept of middle out.

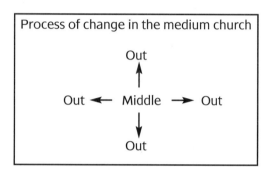

"Excellent!" Bob cheered me on. "All pastors of medium churches should keep that diagram in mind when seeking to initiate changes. Pastors of medium churches should ask, What key groups—committees, boards, task forces, commissions—need to own the change before it can happen? Let's move on to the large church. What does top down mean? It should be fairly obvious."

"I think so," I said. "*Top down* means that in larger churches, changes can be initiated *and* launched by the senior pastor with the assistance of key staff and lay leaders on the governing board. Here's how I'd illustrate that approach to initiating change in a large church."

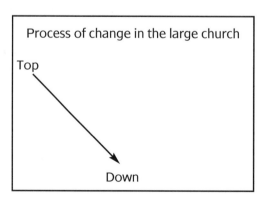

"Right," said my mentor.

"Aha!" I blurted out. "Once you begin to focus on issues in light of church sizes, the answers become fairly obvious."

"Precisely. I do, though, want to caution you about becoming overly simplistic. The ideas summarized in *McIntosh's Typology of Church Sizes* are just prompts for ideas that go much deeper than we've been able to explore. Consider the concept of top down change. At first glance, a pastor may think he can simply tell the church what to do, and people will follow. I call this the Rawhide Rule of Leadership: Don't try to understand them; just drive 'em, rope 'em, and brand 'em. This leadership approach is successful in only rare situations. I always say:

You don't push people; you pull them.

"This approach to leadership works in every size church. It's the Chain Principle of Leadership. If I were to lay a small chain on the table and ask you to move it without lifting it off the table, you would have two choices—push it or pull it. If you tried to push the chain, it would bunch up in a pile as in this drawing." Bob proceeded to draw the picture below.

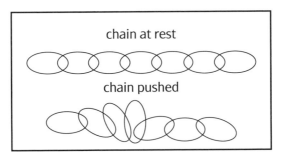

101

"Every time you try to push the chain, it resists by bunching up. Of course, if you keep pushing, after a while the chain does move in the direction you want it to go. However, it's not the most effective way to move the chain. Instead of the links doing their job—each pulling the next one along—they end up in a resistant pile."

"Exactly," I said, nodding my head.

"It's obvious that the most effective way to move the chain is to pull it. By doing so, the links work together to move the chain along, and it actually takes much less energy. If actually practiced, the Chain Principle of Leadership illustrates how an effective pastor leads the flock of God. Shepherds never drove their sheep, they led them. Effective pastors today don't push the sheep, they pull them, regardless of the size church in which they serve."

"I'm afraid I used to do a lot of pushing," I interjected. "Without knowing it, I was using the Rawhide Rule of Leadership—which failed 90 percent of the time. But over the last few weeks, I've started using the Chain Principle of Leadership, and my people are much more receptive.

"How fast should I move forward with changes? I've heard two viewpoints. One says not to change anything during the first year. The other says to change as much as you can in the first year. Which is correct?"

"I suggest that in the early years of ministry in a new church you follow the Law of the Snake Pit:

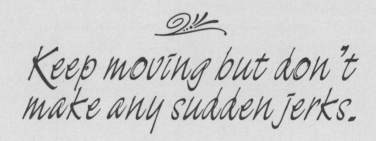

Keep moving but don't make any sudden jerks.

As we chuckled, Bob added, "Another way to put this is Make Haste Slowly. In other words, you want to make enough changes to move the church forward without frightening the people."

"So, how do you know when to make the larger changes?" I asked.

"If God opens a door for change," Bob suggested, "go through it. But wait until he opens a door."

"You said wait until God opens the door. How do I know when that happens?"

"I'll answer your question in a moment," Bob promised, "but let's begin by thinking about the process of change. When you think about it, there is nothing that does *not* change—everything changes. Remember:

> *Change is inevitable, but growth is intentional.*

What we're talking about is not change, which is constantly occurring, but regular, proactive growth of the church's ministry."

"So there is a difference between what we call change and the growth of a church's ministry?"

"That's right," Bob said. "There are actually three levels of change or development in a church: minor change, major change, and transformational change. Minor changes are small modifications made without a corresponding shift in the perception of reality. These minor changes are taking place on a regular basis in all churches, such as when new carpet is installed or the facility is painted. Major changes occur when people develop a new perspective and act in new ways, such as when a church begins to view

103

and treat newcomers as honored guests rather than transient visitors. Transformational change comes only through radical modification in belief and practice, such as when a church reverses an inward focus on believers to an outward focus on the lost."

"That's a good way of explaining change. In my brief experience, it appears that transformational change is what many churches need today."

"A lot of people would agree with you," Bob suggested. "Research on change in various organizations, including churches, has found that the best hope for transformational change is through intentionally following a seven-part process."

While Bob talked, I flipped a page over on my notepad and started listing the seven parts to the *Process of Transformational Change.*

"First, look for teachable moments," Bob began. "The Bible refers to times of opportunity that may never come again. As an example, the apostle Paul reminds us, 'So then, while we have opportunity, let us do good to all men' (Gal. 6:10). We must take advantage of the opportunities to be good to each other because those moments will disappear and may not be available again. In a similar way there are times in a congregation's life when a unique openness arrives that allows transformational change to take place. To answer your earlier question, these are the times when God is opening the doors for change. I've identified five key times during which you should be ready to act. Here's something to help you remember the *Five Opportunities for Change,*" he added as he handed me a small card.

Five Opportunities for Change

1. **A time of crisis.** The crisis may be anything that causes people in the church to announce, "Something must be done." A church fire, the death of a pastor, or the loss of church property to a new highway are all samples of crises that enlarge a congregation's openness to change.

---

2. **A time of pastoral change.** The coming of a new pastor raises questions about the future of the church. It opens the door to discuss the purpose, vision, and goals of the church—all inquiries that force the church to look to the future.

3. **A time of budget preparation.** The annual budget planning process allows the church to rethink its priorities. It can be a time to set new directions and priorities.

4. **A time of revival.** The Holy Spirit occasionally blesses a church with special times of spiritual refreshment. Such moments may follow the prayers of people in the church, but like the wind, we have no sure way of knowing when the Spirit's renewing presence will come. When God does sovereignly touch the life of a church, doors of opportunity open for new approaches to ministry.

5. **A time of planning.** The most common open door for change is created through a normal process of planning. Scheduling a new class or designing a cutting-edge program induces a church to think in new ways. Developing a long-range plan for the future causes a church to review its past, analyze its present, and envision its future.

"I urge you to keep this card handy," Bob encouraged. "If you review it from time to time, you will become sensitive to the opportunities when they come."

"I guess my problem in the past has been in not waiting for the right timing," I admitted. "I've read quite a lot about the need for vision. How does that fit into the process for change?"

"The heart of the change process is the development of a new vision for the future," Bob pressed on. "Thus the second step is to envision a preferable future for the church. In my experience it's been helpful to answer the question, If my church could be all God wanted it to be in five years, what would it look like? The reason I like this question is that it's simple but profound. It encourages me to think into the future, but not so far that I can't imagine what might take place. It puts the focus on improvement by challenging me to think in terms of all it could be. And it stresses the spiritual dynamic by centering on God. The question is not, What do I want the church to be? rather, What does God want the church to be?"

"Could vision be expressed through a purpose statement?" I asked.

"Somewhat," Bob continued. "However, I like to differentiate purpose and vision. In my mind a church's purpose, or what some call a mission statement, explains the biblical reason a church exists. In contrast a vision statement details *how* the purpose statement will be carried out."

"Can you give me an example?"

"Yes. One of the best purpose statements I've run across is this: 'The purpose of our church is to glorify God by finding, keeping, and building people.' This statement reflects the biblical priorities of evangelization, assimilation, and maturation. Notice, however, this purpose statement says nothing about *how* evangelization, assimilation, or maturation will happen. That's where vision comes into the picture. A vision statement fleshes out the purpose statement in real life. It might read, 'It is our vision to establish a Christian preschool for the unchurched families in our community. We will provide an excellent preschool experience for children, present Christ to the entire family in a loving way, encourage families to find a home at our church, and offer creative seminars to help them mature in their faith.' Can you see the difference? This vision statement clearly defines the how, who, and what of the purpose statement. Using this vision statement, the church can set goals and define plans to realize both the purpose and vision statements."

"That's thought-provoking," I said. "I've never understood the differences in the concepts of purpose and vision, but now I do! Once I determine a vision for the future, what's the next step?"

"The third step is to help the people in a church gain ownership of the vision. One of the best ways to accomplish this is to create dissonance. Before people can own a new vision, it's important that they see the need for change. This takes place when dissonance develops between what is and what might be."

"How is dissonance created?"

"A number of years ago the leaders of a church in Denver, Colorado, wanted to instill a new vision for the city into the hearts and minds of their members. As one step in that process, they took all the worshipers at a Sunday morning service on a tour of Denver. They rented enough buses to take the entire contingent and trained tour guides to point out the needs of the city. On the appointed Sunday morning, it was announced that the sermon would be a tour of the city. All those present were asked to move outside and board the buses, after which they went on their tour. By actually showing the church members the needs of the city 'up close and personal,' the leaders created a dissonance between what their church was actually doing and what God was calling them to do. Now I realize not every church can take its congregation on a tour of the city, but it's a good story of what must be done in every church: to help people see the needs and the opportunities that the vision expresses."

"I have a friend who accomplished the same purpose by using video," I shared. "After a fire destroyed several blocks of homes in a neighborhood near the church building, a few church members took home videos of the burned out area, edited it, and then presented it in a worship service. When the video ended, the pastor shared his vision of assisting the victims of the fire. He received overwhelming support."

"Outstanding!" Bob exclaimed. "I'll use that story someday. It's just what I'm talking about. There are many ways to create dissonance, and demonstrating need and opportunities paves the way for church members to own the vision.

"That leads us to the fourth step. An assessment must be made to determine the activities necessary to actualize the vision. This involves a serious analysis of the church's life with a focus on what changes are needed to move the church toward the vision. I like to list the necessary changes under each major ministry area of the church: outreach, worship, assimilation, education, youth, and so forth. Once a list has been developed, I go back and separate the ideas into three categories: short-term, mid-term, and long-term. Items listed under short-term must be accomplished within one to two years. I place any ideas that need to happen in three to five years under mid-term. All other ideas that need to be done but can wait five or more years go under long-term. These items become the goals of the church."

"In other words, you prioritize the actions that must take place to reach the vision."

"Exactly. By listing each goal, I know specifically what to do and can move strategically. As I check off each goal, I move closer to accomplishing the vision. Of course, as I do this, it's important to reframe people's understanding, which is step number five. It's necessary to reinterpret past events to show they are congruent with the new vision. Using my earlier example, a church may desire to start a Christian preschool, but how does that integrate with the church's former commitment to Vacation Bible School? It's important that a leader demonstrate that the new vision carries on the former vision, just in a different manner."

"What you're saying is that a church's new vision must relate to its past?"

"Yes," Bob agreed. "Unless the church is a new church plant, there is always a history that must be reinterpreted in light of the future. I always say that a church needs to

Look back and leap forward.

Look back to honor the significant movements of God in the church in past days, and then leap forward in anticipation of the fresh opportunities and challenges God is giving to the church today."

"What a fantastic concept," I said. "Previously I've tried to ignore the past and just focus on the future. I'll need to rethink my approach. So what are the last two steps?"

"The sixth step is to mobilize support. If the first five steps are completed well, this step almost takes care of itself. Once people connect the needs and the past with the future vision, they will support the desired changes. This is the point where you ask for donations or volunteers or take a vote. Be careful to complete the first steps before you seek to mobilize support or the vision may backfire."

"I've 'been there, done that,'" I joked.

"Then, of course, the seventh step is to initiate the change. Implement your strategies, making sure to monitor progress, evaluate results, and fashion adjustments as necessary."

Here are the notes I scribbled from Bob's outline:

The Process of Transformational Change

1. Look for teachable moments
2. Envision a preferable future for the church
   - Purpose statement: The biblical reason a church exists
   - Vision statement: How the purpose statement is carried out
3. Help the congregation gain ownership of the vision
4. Determine how to actualize the vision
   - Short-term goals
   - Mid-term goals
   - Long-term goals
5. Reframe people's understanding
6. Mobilize support
7. Initiate the change
   - Monitor progress
   - Evaluate results
   - Fashion adjustments

In recent weeks I have put into practice in my own church Bob's insights on the process of change. I have made significant adjustments in my approach to communicating a vision for the future. As a result, the people of my church have been much more open to changes. While most of what we have done so far would fall into the category of minor changes, with a few being major, I am just about ready to begin our first transformational change. Thanks to Bob I have gained the necessary ownership among my people and I am certain my ideas will be accepted. As a result of these recent changes, we have experienced some additions to the church family. However, this has raised some new questions, such as How do churches grow? and Do all churches face the same obstacles to growth? and What are the best strategies for growth? I'll have to talk to Bob about these in the coming weeks.

Taking It Home

I learned a number of helpful facts from Bob this week. Look over my short list below and note some insights from each for your personal life, ministry, or church.

1. The process of change in the small church is bottom up, in the medium church it is middle out, and in the large church it is top down.

   Insight for your life, ministry, or church:

2. The Chain Principle of Leadership says, "You don't push people; you pull them."

   Insight for your life, ministry, or church:

3. The Law of the Snake Pit says, "Keep moving but don't make any sudden jerks."

   Insight for your life, ministry, or church:

4. There are three levels of change: minor changes, major changes, and transformational changes.

   Insight for your life, ministry, or church:

5. Transformational change takes place in churches when they follow a clear seven-part process.

   Insight for your life, ministry, or church:

How Do Churches Grow?

"SITTING IN YOUR OFFICE a few weeks ago," I began, "I noticed a plaque on the wall that read:

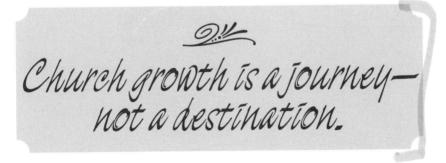

Church growth is a journey— not a destination.

That statement rang true for me. Can you expand on it a little?"

"I think it's good for us to understand that church growth should never be our goal," Bob began. "Church growth is similar to happiness. We never find happiness by searching for it. Happiness is discovered only as a by-product of some other endeavor. As we commit ourselves to our family, work, and a great purpose in life, happiness finds us.

"The same is true for church growth. Ask pastors of larger growing churches how they grew their church and you'll discover many don't have much of an answer. It's as if church growth found them as they pursued a great purpose."

"Wow! I must admit, I've never quite thought of church growth this way. To tell you the truth, I've always harbored more than a few concerns about church growth being just a numbers game."

"No, that's a total misunderstanding," Bob countered. "Church growth is all about making disciples not just adding numbers. Our purpose must always be to make disciples as Christ commanded in Matthew 28:16–20. We must focus on the same purpose as Christ who came to seek and save the lost, as he said in Luke 19:10. It is as we invest our life and energy in the pursuit of this ultimate goal that growth will happen of its own accord as a by-product of our investment. True disciple making results in new disciples finding their way into a relationship with a local church, which, of course, results in church growth."

"That makes sense," I said. "My former church established a rule that when they reached a certain size they would stop growing and spin off a daughter church. Is that a wise choice? Do you think there is a preferable size for a church?"

"Again, that's the reason I like to say, 'Church growth is a journey not a destination,'" Bob explained. "If growth were the destination, we would have a clear target size given in Scripture. God surely would have told us how big he wants churches to get. He would have instructed us to stop growing at a certain size or when to spin off a new congregation.

"Of course, nowhere in the Bible does God give us this sort of information. And, as far as we know, there is no preferable size for a church. I compare a growing church to a growing child. Would any wise parent say to his or her child, 'You're tall enough and your feet are too big. Stop growing'? I don't think so. We don't stop buying our children shoes when their feet reach a certain size. On the contrary, as our children grow, we keep buying larger shoes until our child stops growing naturally."

"If people have a natural size they grow into," I asked, "doesn't it make sense that churches would have a natural size also, a point at which they'd stop growing?"

"Not necessarily," Bob answered. "This is one of those yes and no answers. First, this is where the analogy of a growing child breaks down. While a person does reach a point of maximum growth, a church never does. As long as there are lost people who need to be found and brought to Jesus Christ, the need for church growth will always be valid. While a particular local church may reach a maximum size, it can continue its growth by multiplying new churches. In fact church growth is more about planting new churches than simply enlarging a single church. Our churches must never stop growing. There is no perfect size church. The only perfect church is the one still on the journey—a journey of seeking and saving the lost."

Interrupting Bob's train of thought, I commented, "I take it you believe God wants churches to grow."

"Absolutely!" Bob thundered. "Let me ask you a question. Do you think God wants his church to decline?"

I could tell I had touched a nerve, but I had to admit, "No, I don't think God desires his church to decline."

"Well, consider this question. Does God want his church to plateau?"

I could see where Bob was going with this line of questioning but again I had to grant, "No, I don't think God desires his church to plateau."

"In my mind," Bob continued, "there's no other choice for most churches but to grow. The first clear word our Lord gave concerning the church had to do, not with a definition of it, but with the growth of it! Remember our Lord's words in Matthew 16:18, '. . . I will build My church. . . .' Countless pages of commentary have been written on this verse, but the Bible is its own best commentary. By God's grace the disciples took the lead in a vast program of evangelizing and church building. Those who ministered under the mandate of our Lord did not simply do good works. They preached the gospel, won people to Christ, *and* formed them into churches. Name that task church growth or whatever you like, that is Christ's promise."

"You've convinced me," I laughed. "You said it was a yes and no answer. What's the yes about?"

"The yes part of the answer means there are some limits on how large a church can grow, primarily based on the church's community. Look at this illustration.

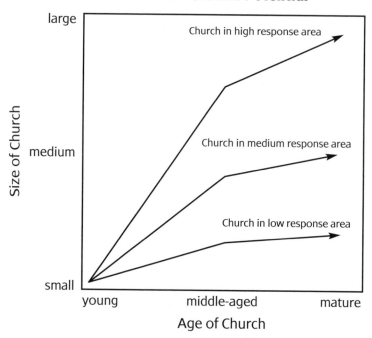

Church Growth Potential

"This chart is a bit simplistic, but it does illustrate several facets of church growth. First, a church's ultimate size is determined to some degree by the responsiveness of the area in which it ministers. A church in a community that isn't responsive has a limited growth potential. It can grow, of course, but it's not likely to grow as large or at the same pace as a church in a high response area. Second, a church's growth potential declines with age. Research on the life cycle of churches reveals that the best years for a church to experience growth are in the first twenty-five years of its life. Older churches can grow, but it becomes more difficult to break out of old patterns to establish a new vision so crucial to growth. Third, almost every church can grow a little, even those in low growth areas."

"Stop right there for a minute and let's unpack that last point," I interrupted. "What do you mean 'almost every church can grow a little'?"

McIntosh's Typology of Church Sizes

Factors	Small Church	Medium Church	Large Church
Size	15–200 worshipers	201–400 worshipers	401+ worshipers
Orientation	Relational	Programmatical	Organizational
Structure	Single cell	Stretched cell	Multiple cell
Leadership	Resides in key families	Resides in committees	Resides in select leaders
Pastor	Lover	Administrator	Leader
Decisions	Made by congregation	Made by committees	Made by staff and leaders
	Driven by history	Driven by changing needs	Driven by vision
Staff	Bivocational or single pastor	Pastor and small staff	Multiple staff
Change	Bottom up through key people	Middle out through key committees	Top down through key leaders
Growth Patterns	Attraction model through relationships	Program model through key ministry	Proclamation model through word of mouth

117

"I mean that virtually every church can grow—make disciples— even if only one or two disciples are won to Christ and assimilated into a church each year. Back in 1990 I read where some researchers expected church membership to increase 3 percent a year. That wouldn't be considered outstanding growth, but it is growth. According to my figures, most churches could grow around 5 percent a year if they retooled and refocused their resources on making disciples. Five percent a year over ten years amounts to 62.5 percent growth. As for the word *almost,* I simply mean there are some churches that possibly cannot grow, even a little. As an example, churches in small, declining communities may find it difficult to grow due to the out-migration of people. However, they should at least have a desire to grow by making disciples."[18]

"Well," I said, "I'd guess my church is in a medium response area, which means we should be able to experience more growth than we have in the last few years." Pointing to *McIntosh's Typology of Church Sizes,* I added, "This seems to indicate that each size church demonstrates defined patterns of growth. I'd like to learn about these patterns: *attraction model, program model,* and *proclamation model.*"

"Several key factors come together to cause people to select a church," Bob observed. "Nevertheless, when we look closely at churches by size, we find each has a particular model for growth.

"Small churches grow through the *attraction model.* Growth through attraction occurs when a church exudes so much warmth and love that newcomers are attracted. Someone called this the Moth Principle of Church Growth:

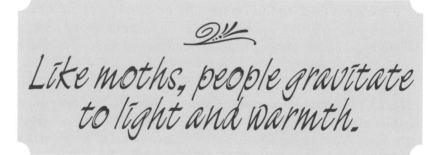

Like moths, people gravitate to light and warmth.

"This model of growth fits well with the small church. As we've talked about in previous discussions, small churches have a relational orientation. If the relationships within a small church are healthy, exuding love and care, the church stands an excellent chance of growing through attraction. Unchurched people rarely shop for a church. They come because they are invited by someone who already attends. When church members reach out in love to their family, friends, and associates, people are attracted to the church."

"It seems to me that a potential weakness of this model, however, is that it reaches only those with some connection to the church. Am I correct?" I asked.

"Yes," my mentor acknowledged, "yet even with this weakness, this is the way small churches initially grow. The Nazarene Church in the United States is an eminent example. A few years ago I read in their *GROW* magazine that they added 30,000 people to their membership rolls. The article mentioned that 25 percent of the new Nazarenes were children from Nazarene families. Another 35 percent of new Nazarenes had extended family or close friends in the congregation they joined. A surprise finding showed that only one new Nazarene in ten had no significant previous ties to the congregation they joined![19] Of further importance is the reality that the Church of the Nazarene is a denomination of small churches. Their research found that average worship attendance was one hundred in active Nazarene churches, and half of the churches had fewer than sixty-five in worship on any given Sunday.[20] The attraction model appears to be the prominent growth strategy for small Nazarene churches, as it is for any small church."

"My church fits into this category," I interjected, "so I'm interested in pursuing this further. I'd say the people in my church demonstrate a good level of love and care toward each other. How can I lead them to share their love with new people?"

"That's part of the challenge of leading the small church," Bob admitted. "First, I recommend you begin by praising your people for this strength. Be glad they are a warm and loving church rather than a sad and fighting one. Second, at an opportune time ask the congregation if God wants them to share their love with others. We know the answer to that question, and so will they. One way to do this is to bring your people together where you can spend two or three hours discussing some relevant questions. Ask everyone present to break into small groups of three to five people. Assign a reporter to each group, then ask each group member to share with the others the answers to the following questions:

1. Why did I visit this church for the first time?
2. Why did I decide to join or become a regular attender?
3. What is special about this congregation?
4. What might a new person gain by being with us?
5. What might our congregation gain by inviting friends to be with us for worship and other activities?
6. Do we really want new people in our congregation?
7. How do we invite friends to visit our congregation?
8. Are newcomers welcome here?
9. Are we ready to be inviting people?
10. How can we begin to share our love with friends outside our church?[21]

"You can divide these questions into sections, but occasionally ask the reporters to tell the entire group what they've learned. It's wise to list the findings of the total group on large sheets of paper taped to a wall. In this way everyone can see the combined thinking of the group. As you sense God's direction in the discussion, move toward a practical decision and commitment from the group. Keep the process simple, realizing that the process is as important as the final decision. Based on our previous talks, help the people see the need and opportunity, but let them decide how to implement the decisions."

"Thanks! That gives me some idea on how to get started. I really believe our church has a lot to give in terms of love and care to outsiders."

"I'm sure they do," Bob concurred. "Now, as a church grows, the new people bring new needs and desires for additional programming. New ministries are developed and, as a rule, at least one of the new programs becomes a star."

"What's a star?"

"Stay with me for a minute and you'll understand," Bob encouraged. "The Pareto Principle, commonly called the 80/20 rule states: 20 percent of your effort gives you 80 percent of your results. I've since learned that this principle may be broken down even further as follows.

- 20% effort = 80% results
- 30% effort = 15% results
- 50% effort = 5% results

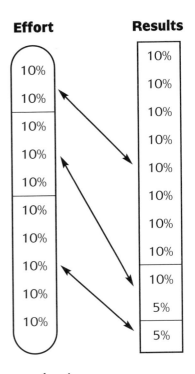

"This means that 20 percent of your members will win 80 percent of your converts, 30 percent of your members will win 15 percent of your converts, and 50 percent of your members will win 5 percent."

"I understand," I said, jumping into the discussion. "As for stewardship, 20 percent of the members will give 80 percent of the money, 30 percent of the members will give 15 percent of the money, and 50 percent will give 5 percent."

"Correct! Now the same holds true for church programs. Twenty percent of your ministries will attract 80 percent of the people, 30 percent of your ministries will attract 15 percent, and 50 percent will attract 5 percent. Your star programs or ministries are the top 20 percent, which produce 80 percent of your growth.

"At first thought, this principle may not seem that important. Yet, the more you think it through, the more you will begin to understand its strategic implications. The chart above will help you visualize the impact of your effort on the end results.

"Looking at the chart from left to right reveals that only a little of what you do produces much in the way of results. For example, time invested in only 20 percent of your activities is usually multiplied fourfold in end results. Looking at the chart from right to left reveals how to invest your resources of time, energy, money, and people. For example, to get the best results, you should invest 80 percent of your resources in the 20 percent of the programs that are the most effective. In this day of limited ministry resources, it's crucial that you put your time, energy, money, and people where they will do the most good.

"A lot of what you read about leadership and church growth is sound advice. However, seldom do you hear about this effective strategy: Concentrate on your stars."

"Okay, I get the idea. Can you give me a real example?" I asked.

"Sure thing," Bob replied. "Remember the vision statement I shared with you last week?"

"You mean the one about starting a Christian preschool?" I asked.

"Yes, that one. The pastor of that church is a close friend of mine. When his church developed that vision statement, the church averaged about 54 people in worship attendance. Over the following eleven years, the church gradually grew until it averaged around 280 attenders at worship. During those years he kept careful records and discovered that 50 percent of the newcomers to the church made their first contact through the preschool. Thirty-three percent of the people he baptized came through the preschool. Twenty-nine percent of the new members came from the preschool. The preschool was his star ministry since it was responsible for most of the new growth in the church."

"This is what's called the *program model?*"

"It is! Medium-sized churches grow as they develop one or two key ministries that effectively reach new people for Christ and bring them into the church."

"That's a good way of putting it," I said. "It makes perfect sense since the medium-sized church has a programmatical orientation."

"It does," Bob agreed. "The *proclamation model* found in larger churches also makes sense. Growth through proclamation occurs when a church heralds the Good News of Christ through many different avenues, effectively winning people to Christ and drawing them to church. This is what happened during the ministry of Christ. Mark records that following one of Jesus' miracles, 'the news about Him went out everywhere into all the surrounding district' (Mark 1:28). The word translated 'news' can also be 'report' or 'rumor.' Today we'd say 'word of mouth.' Jesus' ministry was predominantly communicated by word of mouth. After Jesus raised a dead man, Luke records that 'this report concerning Him went out all over Judea, and in all the surrounding district' (Luke 7:17)."

"So is the proclamation in the large church about Christ or about the church?" I asked.

"Both," Bob said firmly. "The entire model involves a series of proclamations—from the pulpit, in the community, person-to-person. The resources of the larger church allow it to advertise its various programs—another type of proclamation—and generally get the word out about Christ and the church's entire ministry. A classic example of how word-of-mouth proclamation affects a church is found in 1 Thessalonians 1:8. Writing about the church in Thessalonica, Paul says, 'For the word of the Lord has sounded forth from you, not only in Macedonia and Achaia, but also in every place your faith toward God has gone forth.' People were telling how the Thessalonians had turned from idols to serve the living and true God. They were spreading the story by word of mouth. It was so effective that Paul confesses 'we have no need to say anything.'"

"Can't the growth of large churches be attributed to the exceptional speaking of the senior pastor?" I inquired.

"Sometimes it appears that way," Bob agreed, "but when we dig deeper, we discover that the growth of large churches is more in the control of the people than of the pastor. Studies in the field of diffusion of innovation, or how new products spread, have found that people do not choose a product purely on factual information. The overwhelming majority of people depend on subjective evaluations conveyed to them from other individuals like themselves who have previously used a product. New products literally take

123

off after interpersonal networks are activated to spread subjective, positive word of mouth."

"I can testify to that fact," I shared. "When my wife and I first arrived in town, we asked around to find a doctor, a hairdresser, and many other services. We made most of our choices based on what people told us."

"We all make decisions that way," Bob confirmed. "Large churches grow in a similar manner as members and attenders proclaim good word-of-mouth evaluations to their friends, family, and associates. The spreading talk develops an 'echo effect' as word of mouth reverberates back and forth, spilling over to other people who may be interested in the church."

"All churches depend on word-of-mouth proclamation to some degree don't they?"

"That's for sure. To some extent, every size church practices all the models we've discussed. But churches grow best when they focus on their strengths. The numerous resources found in the larger church make a proclamation approach workable. Large churches have natural word-of-mouth exposure due to the number of people who participate in their ministry. They have the financial base to proclaim through advertising. On the other hand, the limited resources of the smaller church mean less impact through a proclamational approach. Small churches grow best as they focus on the attraction model, which builds on their strengths."

"And . . . medium churches grow best as they develop new ministries to meet the relevant needs of the new people they're attempting to reach."

"I think you've got it!"

Taking It Home

A lot has happened since I learned about the growth patterns of different size churches. I have focused more on helping my church members attract their friends and family to Christ by extending their love outside the church family. What growth pattern do you see functioning in your church? As I discovered, all churches have some aspects of each model even though we lean toward one of the three. List below the aspects of each growth model you see in your church today.

Attraction Model:

Program Model:

Proclamation Model:

What Are the
Obstacles to Growth?

My discussion with Bob haunted me all week. Living things grow. Trees grow. Children grow. Faith grows. Growth is a biblical concept. When something that is supposed to grow does not grow, we wonder why. My church was not growing and it disturbed me.

During the week I mulled over the fact that the few visitors who venture into our worship service rarely return. Walking from the parsonage to the church building each Sunday morning provides me with a good view of the parking lot. I always know we have visitors when there is a different car in the lot. When visitors do come, our church appears friendly enough. People go out of their way to talk to the visitors as they enter the building. Each week I send out around five letters to visitors, which, for a small church like ours, is a good number. I wondered why nearly all of our visitors fail to return for a second visit.

I had learned a lot from my mentor over the past two months. So naturally at our next meeting, I decided to bring up the question of why my church was not growing. It was too bad Bob and I did not have time to go away on a retreat for a few days to discuss many of these issues at length. Meeting every week, however, was probably best because it gave me time to digest what we discussed.

A warm rain was coming down as Bob arrived for our weekly discussion. He arrived at 7:30 sharp. After we exchanged cordial greetings, I shared my frustration about visitors who come but do not return.

"Sounds like you're ready to move on to the next phase of our discussion," Bob encouraged.

"What's that?" I asked.

"Barriers!"

"Barriers?"

"Yes," Bob emphasized. "Barriers, or growth obstacles. All churches have barriers or obstacles that exclude people."

"What do you mean churches exclude people?" I asked a little indignantly. "My church is open to anyone who wants to come."

"I'm not surprised you feel that way," Bob replied. "Nearly all church members feel their church is open, friendly, and accepting. A few years ago I was asked to share the story of my church's growth with several small congregations. Each time I spoke, I asked the people to tell me the best thing about their own church. The number one answer each church gave was We're a friendly church. Of course, the interesting fact was that none of those churches was growing."

"Sounds a lot like my church," I admitted.

"No church excludes people on purpose," Bob continued. "Yet, the truth is there are numerous obstacles or barriers to a church's growth. Some of these are invisible but many can be seen if we look for them. Let me give you some examples. Some visitors may see the name of the church as a barrier. Perhaps they experienced the pain of rejection in a previous church with a similar name. The name of the church may remind them of their personal hurt and it is an invisible barrier that must be removed before they can settle into a church. A visible barrier that is common in older churches is a stairway. Numerous steps are obstacles to some people who might attend church."

"I can identify with that obstacle," I declared. "The fellowship hall in my church is located in the basement and the only way to get there is down a long flight of stairs. A few of our people don't come to church fellowships because the stairs are too difficult to manage."

"Yes," my mentor agreed, "and without knowing it, your church excludes those who can't manage the stairs. Fortunately churches have become more aware of physical barriers and are taking steps to remove them.

"The list of obstacles is far longer and more complex than most members realize. The two of us could list quite a number of obstacles to a church's growth, but since we don't have much time today, let's look at the card I gave you of *McIntosh's Typology of Church Sizes*. You'll see that McIntosh summarizes five growth obstacles for each size church."

At that point, my mentor reviewed the five obstacles for each size church. "Before I summarize each of these obstacles," Bob cautioned, "it's important to remember that just as God has not created any two people exactly alike, no two congregations are photocopies either. However, there are enough similarities among churches that common barriers to their growth and development are easily listed according to size. At this point let's just look over the obstacles and we can talk about strategies for growth next time we meet."

With Bob's caution in mind, I will now briefly run through each obstacle as he did with me.

Obstacle 1 for smaller churches is a *small-church image*. Studies suggest that a primary difference between growing and declining churches is their attitude. Growing churches feel they have something worthwhile to offer to their community. Their high level of

McIntosh's Typology of Church Sizes

Factors	Small Church	Medium Church	Large Church
Size	15–200 worshipers	201–400 worshipers	401+ worshipers
Orientation	Relational	Programmatical	Organizational
Structure	Single cell	Stretched cell	Multiple cell
Leadership	Resides in key families	Resides in committees	Resides in select leaders
Pastor	Lover	Administrator	Leader
Decisions	Made by congregation Driven by history	Made by committees Driven by changing needs	Made by staff and leaders Driven by vision
Staff	Bivocational or single pastor	Pastor and small staff	Multiple staff
Change	Bottom up through key people	Middle out through key committees	Top down through key leaders
Growth Patterns	Attraction model through relationships	Program model through key ministry	Proclamation model through word of mouth
Growth Obstacles	Small-church image Ineffective evangelism Inadequate programming Downward momentum Ingrown fellowship	Inadequate facilities Inadequate staff Inadequate finances Poor administration Increasing complexity	Poor assimilation Increased bureaucracy Poor communication Loss of vision Lack of member care

self-esteem provides the energy and strength to share the gospel of Christ with people in the community. Declining churches, unfortunately, believe they are too small to give anything of significance to the people in their community. Thus they retreat into a protective shell and fail to penetrate their community with Christ's love.

The small-church image results in a low level of congregational morale, which creates the feeling, We could never do that! or That would never work here! Low morale is often created when:

- Leaders set the church up for failure by establishing unreachable goals.
- Victories are not celebrated.
- Leaders lose the trust of the congregation.
- Churchwide decisions are manipulated.
- Promises are left unfulfilled.

My mentor gave me a card with the title *Ten Signs of Positive Self-Esteem*. He encouraged me to evaluate my own church's self-image by placing a check mark beside the points that were true of my church. Bob said that seven or more check marks indicate a church that has a healthy self-image, three or fewer checks mean its self-image is dangerously low. Six checks or fewer is cause for concern.

Ten Signs of Positive Self-Esteem
1. Members feel good about their church.
2. Members want others to experience their church.
3. Members get involved in the life of their church.
4. Members look to the future more than the past.
5. Members are willing to take reasonable risks.
6. Members take pride in maintaining their church facilities.
7. Members feel their church is something special.
8. Members are constantly affirmed by their leaders.
9. Members set high standards for excellence.
10. Members have vision for the future.

Obstacle 2 for smaller churches is *ineffective evangelism*. Many, not all, small churches find it difficult to win people to Christ. Low self-esteem causes them to withdraw rather than reach out intentionally to lost people with the love of Christ. This results in small churches evangelizing only their immediate families and a few people whom they "adopt" into the family or relying solely on the pastor to reach new people for Christ. None of these approaches to evangelism is effective over the long haul. It is not unkind to say that the ingrownness of many congregations is the antithesis of the Great Commission to make disciples.

Small churches are often victims of a bigger is better mentality, which leads them to believe they are less capable of evangelizing their unchurched community. The truth is actually the opposite. Small churches can be extremely effective in outreach. Surveys among non-Christians reveal that they tend to have relational concerns: Are the people friendly? Will I be accepted if I don't dress up? Will I meet people who are like me and who will like me? Will I feel guilty or put down or bored or out of place? The relational orientation of the small church makes it a prime place for non-Christians to find Christ. However, the small church must refocus its evangelism efforts. In order to overcome this barrier, it must develop three aspects of ministry: a sense of mission, a sense of urgency, and an open fellowship.

Obstacle 3 for small churches is *inadequate programming*. Every pastor of a small church has experienced the sadness of losing people due to the lack of programming. Parents of teenagers often leave a small church to find a larger church with an active youth program. Musicians leave smaller churches to become involved in a church offering a greater variety of music. Creative people move to other churches to find additional outlets for their new approaches to ministry.

A contributing factor to inadequate programming in small churches is the cutback syndrome. Limited resources encourage small churches to put a premium on efficiency and economy. With the best of intentions, leaders cut back on staff, programs, maintenance, and outreach to save the church money. Regrettably, cutting back to save money reduces potential for reaching new people and assimilating them into the church. Thus the small church grows smaller or remains on a stagnant plateau.

Obstacle 4 for small churches is *downward momentum*. If you can remember a time when you removed the plug in the bottom of a sink full of water, you will comprehend this obstacle. Once the downward pull of the water begins, everything goes with it. This is precisely the case in many small churches, particularly those that have declined from a larger size. Once a church begins declining, retreating inward, and cutting back on ministry, it becomes next to impossible for the church to focus on anything but survival. That is why the number one priority for many smaller churches is survival. They bury their talents in the ground to save and protect what they have. Caught in the vortex pulling them ever downward, the people begin to wonder why God does not bless them with more. They forget that God has already blessed them abundantly but they must invest their talents rather than seek to preserve them.

Obstacle 5 for the small church is *ingrown fellowship*. This obstacle may be the primary one confronting small churches. As a general rule during the first seven to ten years of a church's life span, it has good success at reaching, attracting, and assimilating newcomers. However, the longer a church remains small, and the longer it is in existence, the more ingrown the fellowship structures become. The normal fellowship structures—groups, classes, circles—become so full they can no longer absorb outsiders. If the church has a high age profile, i.e., the people in the congregation are older, the ingrownness can be heightened. People tend to develop most of their skills for building friendships during their younger years. Going to school, relocating to new neighborhoods, taking a first job, joining a new organization, involving children in athletic activities, and other similar events encourage people to develop and use friendship-building skills. As the years pass and people work at one job, reside in the same home, and settle into a comfortable church, they gradually withdraw from building friend-

133

ships with strangers. Thus the longer a church has been in existence and the older the people in the church are, the more likely the church will be ingrown.

This description helped me understand what was taking place in my own church. Newcomers come and go, but few stay long enough to be accepted into the fellowship structures of my church. Visualize a sponge that is so full of water it cannot absorb any more and you will have a good picture of what my small church was experiencing.

My mentor told me there are usually three key indicators present when a church is ingrown.

1. More than 50 percent of the members have been in the congregation twelve or more years.
2. More than 33 percent of the members of the governing board are related to the main families in the church.
3. Fewer than 10 percent of the members have come in the last year.

Churches where all three of these indicators exist are extremely ingrown and will find it difficult to attract and keep newcomers in their congregation.

Becoming aware of these obstacles to growth in a small church allowed me to view my church from a much wiser perspective. Now that I know where the blockages are, it will be much easier to design a strategy to remove them in the coming years.

Bob continued to describe the growth obstacles found in medium-sized churches. Again I will summarize his comments for you.

Obstacle 1 for the medium church is *inadequate facilities*. All sizes of churches could and probably do identify with the lack of facilities. However, this is a particular obstacle for medium-sized churches, particularly if they have experienced a recent growth spurt. As my mentor had discussed in one of our earlier conversations, some medium-sized churches are transitioning from a small church to a large one. Their growth into a medium-sized church places major pressure on all ministries as they try to fit everything into a small facility. The answer is obvious, but medium-sized churches usually find it difficult to purchase new property on which to build or to remodel their current facility, since their growth is already straining the church budget.

Obstacle 2 for the medium church is *inadequate staff.* Today's congregations expect a high quality and diverse ministry. Their desire to have a broad range of specialized programs, worship services, and groups usually leaves a church understaffed. At the core, a medium-sized church has three options: Add sufficient staff to continue growing, add just enough staff to remain plateaued at its present level of attendance, or do not add staff and face eventual decline. Once again the awkward nature of the medium-sized church comes into play as additional staff are needed but the competing needs sometimes do not leave enough in the budget to hire the new staff.

A related need is what pastors in medium churches see as their major problem—motivating and recruiting volunteers. Back in the 1950s, a significant number of volunteers, the highest percentage of which were women, staffed volunteer organizations, particularly in churches. As more and more women have entered the work force during the past half century, there has been a corresponding lack of volunteers for church ministry. Most people who have full-time employment can give no more than three to eight hours a week to church activities. If three or four hours are used on Sunday, only a few hours are available for other volunteer ministries during the week. Careful use of volunteers in all churches, but especially medium-sized ones, is crucial for ongoing growth. Mobilizing lay volunteers is a needed ministry at any level but it rises to the top for medium churches. At best, many medium churches will be able to hire only enough paid pastoral staff to remain on a plateau. To keep advancing, they must find a way to involve laypersons in effective ministry. This usually means:

- placing a high value on laypersons
- developing a workable way to identify the gifts, talents, and skill of laypersons

- placing laypersons in acceptable places of service
- coaching laypersons throughout their service
- putting in place a leadership team to oversee the service of laypersons

Obstacle 3 for the medium church is *inadequate finances*. Every church can identify with this obstacle. If we only had additional money, we could . . . is commonly heard among churches of all sizes. Yet the need for managed stewardship, fund-raising, and professional handling of church funds is crucial for a church at this stage of development. The need for enlarged facilities, additional staff, program expansion, and resources to carry on a growing ministry are rarely more complex than at this stage.

Obstacle 4 for the medium church is *poor administration*. Small churches do not require a sophisticated level of management. But as a church grows into the middle stage, the pastor, staff, and leaders must care effectively for the increasingly complex functional needs of the church. The typical management problems that surface in this size church include but are not limited to:

- confusing "means" with "ends"
- lack of planning and coordination
- ineffective time management
- poor use of volunteers
- poor budget control

Obstacle 5 for the medium church is *increasing complexity*. The increased level of complexity is one of the factors that causes churches to revert to a small church after a few years at medium size. Long-term members may recall the "simple" atmosphere of the small church. The increased complexity that requires them to make an appointment with the pastor, reserve a room for a potluck meal, or budget for next year is not appreciated. They would prefer a simpler structure and will do what they can to return the church to previous times, if they get a chance.

After a few years of growth, the medium-sized congregation must make the necessary adjustments to move to the next size church or it will plateau. Medium churches that plateau are always in great danger of declining, due to the pressure to eliminate the complexity by simplifying and reducing the program, staff, and budget.

Large churches face obstacles also. The following five tend to be the major ones that undermine their ministry.

Obstacle 1 for the large church is *poor assimilation.* Large churches find it unusually easy to attract visitors to the numerous events and activities that take place each week. The challenge is not to attract more people but to assimilate those who come into the life of the congregation. As a general rule, smaller congregations can effectively assimilate new people using informal friendship processes. However, the larger a church grows, the more necessary it becomes to structure mundane procedures for welcoming, following up, and involving visitors. Any attitude that suggests "we'll meet visitors halfway" will result in few newcomers becoming involved in the life of the church. If larger congregations are to assimilate newcomers well, they must go farther than halfway by designing and communicating a clear, precise process for involving newcomers in the life of the church.

Obstacle 2 for the large church is *increased bureaucracy.* Churches that experience growth from small to medium to large may become paralyzed. Organizational structures and processes that worked when the church was smaller become dysfunctional with a larger congregation. Bob noted that the worst situation he had ever heard of was a church in Kentucky that had sixty-one different committees. The committee system worked well when the church was medium-sized, but after it grew, the main work of the committees was just trying to keep from bumping into each other. The committees spent most of their time trying to justify their existence. After a new pastor arrived, he convinced the leaders that the old committee system had become so inept it demanded more than it was providing. Over the next nine years the church designed a new system. Today the 2,200-member congregation has only three committees: worship, ministry, and mission. For large churches to continue growing, they must design and implement a simple structure in which members of the governing board become cheerleaders for the staff, who make the everyday decisions, and laypersons, who minister with their gifts.

Obstacle 3 for the large church is *poor communication.* Communication in small churches takes place through personal relationships along what is called the grapevine. In the majority of smaller churches this approach to communication works fairly well. It provides a fast and reasonably accurate vehicle to communicate with members. As one can guess, however, the larger a church becomes, the less effective this informal communication system is. The more scattered the congregation and the larger the geographical community, the greater the decrease in the speed and accuracy of the grapevine. Effective communication in larger churches requires two main ingredients: redundancy and numerous channels. Generally, a large church should use a minimum of five different channels for any important communication. These channels could include a prayer chain, the church newsletter, Sunday announcements, personal letters, and phone calls. Information should be communicated through such channels over and over and over again.

Obstacle 4 for the large church is *loss of vision.* Healthy, growing churches begin with a challenging dream. But by the time many large churches reach their peak attendance, the dream that propelled them to growth and vitality has likely been realized. When the sense of primary vision has been lost, a large church can easily slide into a maintenance mentality. Gradually inordinate amounts of physical energy and financial resources are directed toward maintenance of the institutional aspects of the church. The resulting comfort and complacency eventually stall the church's desire to make disciples. The answer? Larger churches must dream a new dream for their future and communicate it to the congregation.

Obstacle 5 for the large church is *lack of member care.* A fact that large churches ignore is that they already have more people than they can care for adequately. Placing the total responsibility for member care on the shoulders of the pastoral staff often results in low levels of personal satisfaction among worshipers. To overcome this obstacle, large churches must develop a healthy infrastructure of medium- and small-sized groups where members can be cared for at a personal level.

For good member care to take place, a large church needs approximately three medium-sized groups or classes ranging between twenty to sixty people for every hundred adults at worship. The importance of these medium-sized groups is to provide people with a place where they can know and be known by others. Studies confirm that the average church member can call approximately sixty people by first name, regardless of the size of the church. Given this fact, a person's involvement with other people has little to do with church size but a lot to do with the size of the class or group in which he or she becomes involved.

Then for maximum member care, a larger church needs an additional six or seven small groups ranging in size from three to twenty people for every hundred adults. It is in the small groups and classes that highly personal, intimate care takes place. "To grow large we have to grow small" must be the battle cry of all large churches if they are to maintain healthy relationships among their people.

As I drove home from my meeting with Bob, I was overwhelmed with the obstacles facing churches. Actually I was glad I needed to deal with only one set of barriers at a time. My mentor's last words intrigued me

The future of any size church is the sum of its next moves.

If I understood Bob correctly, he was telling me the future health of a church depends on the strategies it develops and implements. I was already looking forward to next week's meeting about growth strategies.

Taking It Home

Bob had asked me an interesting question: "What squeaks?" He reminded me of the proverb, "The squeaky wheel gets the oil." He meant that some obstacles actually "squeak" or make themselves visible. Based on Bob's analysis of the various obstacles found in small, medium, and large churches, which ones "squeak" loudest in your church?

11

What Are the Strategies for Growth?

SITTING IN MY OFFICE after my last breakfast meeting with Bob, I realized my life had taken a sharp turn for the better. While I knew I had a lot more to learn, I had obviously come a long way since that first frustrated call to my mentor.

During the remainder of the week, Bob's last comment persistently came to mind: "The future of any size church is the sum of its next moves."

After all my meetings, discussions, and "aha" moments, it came down to one question, What do I do next?

By now I understood the basic characteristics of small, medium, and large churches. It was finally time to think about strategy, plans, and goals. What steps should I take to enable my church to face the future in a healthy manner?

In the past I had spent a lot of time fighting fires at church. Now I had the opportunity to prevent future fires by developing an effective strategy for growth. It was time for me to manage rather than be managed. It was time to lead rather than be led. Actually I was frightened more by the potential for success than failure. What would happen if my plans worked?

Next to Bob's habit of drawing charts and pictures to illustrate his ideas, he loved to tell stories, which is exactly how he began our next meeting.

"I remember spending summers at my grandfather's farm in Nebraska," Bob began. "Grandpa did his best to make a farmer out of me, but I guess I was too much of a city boy. It was fun, though, to tag along as my grandfather went through his routine of plowing, fertilizing, planting, weeding, spraying, watering, and harvesting. You know," he looked straight at me, "after all his work, Grandpa always gave the credit for the harvest to God. In fact I can't recall ever hearing of a farmer claiming he grew the crop. Farmers either thank God or Mother Nature for blessings."

"You'll get no argument from me," I said. "So what's the point?"

"The point is,

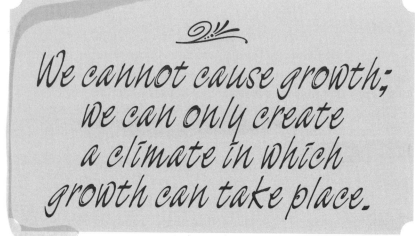

We cannot cause growth; we can only create a climate in which growth can take place.

"Whether it's farming or growing a church, ultimately only God causes the growth. Our responsibility is to do the plowing, planting, watering, fertilizing, weeding, and spraying."

"Isn't that essentially what the apostle Paul said in 1 Corinthians 3:6?" I asked.

"Yes," my mentor agreed as he pulled his Bible out of his briefcase and turned to the passage. "Paul said, 'I planted, Apollos watered, but God was causing the growth.'"

"That balances with what Jesus said when he told his disciples, 'The harvest is plentiful, but the workers are few,' doesn't it?"

"Great insight!" Bob encouraged. "The harvest *is* plentiful because God has caused it to ripen, but he needs workers to work in his harvest field. The workers are called to plant, water, and bring in the harvest God has prepared. It's hard work but eternally satisfying."

"So we need to work harder. Is that the formula for growth?" I pressed.

"Not really," Bob disagreed. "The old saying is true. We need to work smarter, not harder, which brings us to the next row of *McIntosh's Typology of Church Sizes.*"

McIntosh's Typology of Church Sizes

Factors	Small Church	Medium Church	Large Church
Size	15–200 worshipers	201–400 worshipers	401+ worshipers
Orientation	Relational	Programmatical	Organizational
Structure	Single cell	Stretched cell	Multiple cell
Leadership	Resides in key families	Resides in committees	Resides in select leaders
Pastor	Lover	Administrator	Leader
Decisions	Made by congregation Driven by history	Made by committees Driven by changing needs	Made by staff and leaders Driven by vision

Factors	Small Church	Medium Church	Large Church
Staff	Bivocational or single pastor	Pastor and small staff	Multiple staff
Change	Bottom up through key people	Middle out through key committees	Top down through key leaders
Growth Patterns	Attraction model through relationships	Program model through key ministry	Proclamation model through word of mouth
Growth Obstacles	Small-church image Ineffective evangelism Inadequate programming Downward momentum Ingrown fellowship	Inadequate facilities Inadequate staff Inadequate finances Poor administration Increasing complexity	Poor assimilation Increased bureaucracy Poor communication Loss of vision Lack of member care
Growth Strategies	Renew a sense of purpose Begin new ministries Cultivate evangelism Celebrate victories Start new groups/classes Involve new people	Develop distinct identity Add additional staff Use facilities multiple times Offer multiple worship services Write a long-range plan Improve quality of ministry	Renew the vision Design assimilation plan Streamline procedures Offer need-based events Adjust leadership roles Increase the number of small groups

"Working smarter means in part that we work from a basic plan rather than haphazardly. Of course, every church has its own particular set of obstacles and opportunities that may take unique

approaches. However, there are general strategies commonly helpful to each size church."

As we continued our breakfast, Bob and I talked about the six
major growth strategies for each size church. Here is what he told
me concerning small churches.

Growth strategy 1 for small churches is to *renew a sense of purpose.* This begins by focusing the attention of the congregation on
Jesus Christ, particularly his death on the cross. Asking and answering questions such as, What was he doing there? What drove him
to Calvary? What was Christ's purpose? will remind people that
Jesus came to seek and save the lost. Helping the congregation see
that Jesus Christ passed on that purpose to the church is the first
step in renewing a sense of purpose. The next step is to write a new
purpose statement in fresh language and then establish it in the
minds and hearts of the congregation through preaching and teaching in small groups, committee meetings, and one-on-one.

Focusing on a renewed sense of purpose restores a healthy, out-
ward-focused viewpoint. It gives a small church a sense of hope
and motivates members with a sense of direction. It encourages the
congregation to spotlight mission and ministry over nurture and
exclusive relationships.

Growth strategy 2 for small churches is to *begin new ministries.*
The ingrown fellowship in small churches is perpetuated by programs and ministries that have become saturated. Since most people prefer to be in on the ground floor of a new venture, beginning
new ministries is an essential step to attract and hold newcomers.

At first the idea of beginning new ministries sounds impossible
to the small church, but it need not be troubling. "Slow and steady"
is a good slogan to follow. A small church need add only one new
ministry each year to remain open to new persons.

It is a good idea to develop new ministries around the three Es—
events, experiences, and education. For example, a seminar could be
offered to help people going through a life event such as the "empty
nest." A divorce recovery workshop might be started for people experiencing that life trauma. Of course, any number of ministries could

be added focusing on educational interests. A good question for small churches to consider is, Are there any felt needs in our community that we could meet by starting a new ministry? Bob believes:

> *If we don't meet people's felt needs, we will never meet their real needs.*

So if a small church can begin a new ministry to address a particular felt need in its community, it can reach new people.

A crucial aspect of adding new ministries is adding a second worship service. Perhaps the number one way that a small church breaks out of its single cell orientation into a multiple cell orientation is by adding a second worship service. In addition, multiple worship services aid the growth of a small church by

- providing options
- expanding space
- increasing the church's faith
- enlarging ministry
- reaching new people

Growth strategy 3 for small churches is to *cultivate evangelism.* It is rare to find a small church effectively involved in outreach without the personal efforts of the pastor. Therefore, it is vital that the pastor of a small church be alert to opportunities to win people to Christ. Pastors of small churches do well to focus on the times when people are most receptive to Christ through the small church ministry, such as when there is

- a death of a family member
- a personal or family illness
- a need for pastoral counseling
- a child ready for Sunday school
- a wedding

However, the most important dynamic for evangelism, especially in the small relational church, is participation by laypersons. Since the growth of small churches is directly dependent on the adoption of new people into the church family by long-term members, the involvement of laypersons on the front lines of evangelism is crucial.

One approach to evangelism that is usually unsuccessful in small churches is the training class. Bob told me the story of how he tried to train the church members for evangelism when his church was smaller. Apparently he announced from the pulpit that evangelism training would begin on Tuesday evening. When the time arrived, only three people were present—Bob, one deacon, and Bob's wife. With tongue in cheek Bob said, "And my wife was there only to support *me!*"

Bob explained that a better approach is to first, find one or two key people who are interested in reaching new people for Christ. Second, train them in a small peer group as Christ did his disciples. Third, assist the congregation in developing an evangelism consciousness through the preaching and teaching ministry. Fourth, retool one or two traditional ministries so they have more of an outward focus. Bob said his church had taken the traditional Thanksgiving dinner fellowship in November and retooled it to be a harvest dinner targeted toward people outside the church. Fifth, challenge church members to make a prayer list of unchurched friends or family and then pray for the people on their list for an entire year. Sixth, establish a group or class focused solely on outreach. Seventh, develop two or three outreach events a year where church members may bring the people they have been praying for over the year.

Growth strategy 4 for small churches is to *celebrate victories.* Good things are happening in small churches. Unfortunately the low self-image of most small churches leads them to see their weaknesses rather than their strengths. One solution to improve self-esteem in the small church is to call attention to the positives in the church.

Bob told me a story of one church that did this in a creative manner. A small, thirty-five-member church decided to upgrade its parking lot from gravel to asphalt pavement. For three years, the members worked together to raise enough money to complete the project. After more car washes, aluminum can collections, and creative fund-raisers than they wanted to count, the financial goal was reached and the parking lot paved. To celebrate what was undoubtedly a significant victory for such a small group of people, a Christian tailgate party was hosted on the newly paved parking lot. Members, friends, and family came together on a Saturday to celebrate the victory by having a barbecue on the parking lot. Later that day, everyone gathered together for a prayer of thanks and dedication for the Lord's faithfulness. The church's self-esteem went up remarkably.

The application is obvious. Find some positive aspects of your church and celebrate them. Report the results of your effective ministries. Talk about your strengths rather than your weaknesses. Give God praise for each victory. In this way you not only recognize the work of the Lord in your church but reinforce your growth priorities.

Growth strategy 5 for small churches is to *start new groups and classes.*

Many, if not most, small churches are characterized by two circles—a membership circle and a fellowship circle. Newcomers are usually welcomed in the first but find resistance when trying to enter the second. Frequently new people discover they cannot be accepted into this inner fellowship circle until they have spent several years in the church. As frustrations set in, nearly all the new people leave before the circle opens up to them.

To turn this obstacle into an opportunity for growth, a small church must take seriously the truth that:

New units bring new growth.

The creation of new groups and classes begins the process of moving from a single cell church to a multiple cell model of ministry. Rather than trying to fight their way into being accepted by people who have been together for years, new people prefer to join a new group, class, or circle. Typically, more than two-thirds of new classes, groups, or circles are made up of people who were not previously in any group. New units must be started but several do not have to be added all at once. For example, a small church that has only one Sunday school class for adults might add an additional class the first year. Then it could add a third adult class the following year.

Growth strategy 6 for small churches is to *involve new people.* It is a common, but false, assumption that new members or regular attenders in small churches quickly develop a sense of belonging. In reality it takes significant involvement in the life of the church before new members and attenders begin to feel like they really belong. The problem is that rather than involving newcomers in ministry roles or tasks, usually the church does not allow them to serve in any significant way.

A major part of the problem is directly related to the single cell family orientation found in most small churches. Long-term mem-

bers of small churches establish an informal and unspoken proba-
tion period for newcomers. Until a newcomer has proven himself
or herself, involvement in key positions or ministries is withheld.
This results in boards, committees, and ministry teams that are
ingrown, ineffective, and redundant.

To bridge the gap between membership and a sense of belonging, small churches need to focus on involving newcomers as quickly
as possible, but always within six months. If newcomers do not
become involved within that time period, they likely will become
passive or leave altogether. Bob recommended that a small church
set a goal to involve 90 percent of the newcomers within six months
of their first visit.

All of these strategic ideas for the small church made perfect
sense to me. I could see ways to begin applying them immediately
in my own church. Of course, Bob was not finished with his suggestions and continued on to discuss strategies for medium and
large churches.

Growth strategy 1 for medium churches is to *develop a distinct
identity.* Medium churches need to build on their key ministries to
form a distinct identity in the community. Studies have found that
healthy churches of this size usually have at least one ministry for
which they are legendary in their community. Some are thought of
as the church with the excellent preschool. Others are known for
their vibrant worship service. Still others are known for their caring seniors group.

To help identify their uniqueness, medium-sized churches should
ask questions like:

How do most visitors first hear of our church?

What ministries are most effective in bringing new people to
our church?

Which ministry is our star?

For what are we known in the larger community?

Once a medium church identifies the ministry for which it is known in its community, it should begin to highlight that ministry intentionally both within and without. The increased name recognition and visibility will attract even more people to the medium church.

Growth strategy 2 for medium churches is to *add additional staff.* A failure to add additional staff and thus expect the pastor and perhaps a secretary to supervise the entire church program will result in plateau or decline.

The second pastoral staff person should be hired before the church reaches two hundred worshipers on an average Sunday morning. To keep growing, a medium church ought to hire a third pastor just as the church peaks at three hundred worshipers. By adding the third pastoral staff person at this point, the church will have the best chance of moving beyond the four hundred attendance barrier. Following this hiring pattern throughout the life of the church will ensure that the ministry has an excellent chance of expansion.

Support staff is an additional need in a growing medium-sized church. The value of secretaries, maintenance workers, janitors, interns, and various assistants cannot be underestimated. Again research has revealed that a church needs to have a minimum, but probably more, of one support person for every two pastoral staff. Thus one secretary should be hired for two pastors or two secretaries for four pastors. This assumes that the secretarial support staff is primarily assigned to the pastoral staff, which is rarely the case. A growing church will actually come closer to having a one-to-one ratio of support staff to pastoral staff, especially if all support staff such as janitors are included in the count.

Growth strategy 3 for medium churches is to *use facilities multiple times.* Perhaps a more interesting way to title this growth strategy is Dethrone Edifice Rex. Growing medium-sized churches eventually discover they are out of space. One obvious answer is to purchase land and build a new church facility. However, this choice may lead to mortgage payments that strangle a church budget, making finances unavailable for other needs, such as hiring staff. As a general rule, when 50 percent or more of the church budget goes for mortgage payments, utilities, and maintenance, the people become servants of the building. As my mentor told me:

Complex building projects often result in a building complex.

A better answer for most medium churches is to use their facilities multiple times. Multiple worship services, Sunday schools, and other ministries allow a church to

- break free from a plateau
- reach new people
- increase income without increasing expenses
- boost overall attendance
- add new units
- offer a diverse ministry
- involve more people

In addition, remaining in a more modest facility empowers a church to do these three important things:

1. retain the advantages of a small church while enjoying the resources of a big church
2. help people stay visible to each other
3. keep things up close and personal

Growth strategy 4 for medium churches is to offer *multiple worship services*. While most medium churches already have a second worship service, some are now adding three, four, and even five services on nights not normally used for worship in Protestant churches.

Bob's advice to medium churches is to delay building a new worship center until the church has three to four worship services in its present building. By waiting to enter a new building project, the church will have a larger and stronger base to support a building project when the time eventually comes to begin one. But, and perhaps more important, having multiple services extends the medium church further into the realm of the multiple cell orientation. The more multiple celled the medium church becomes, the less likely it will fall prey to the effects of the stretched cell.

Medium churches should give serious consideration to not only adding multiple worship services but to adding multiple congregations. While certainly there are exceptions, most pastors have the physical and emotional energy to preach only three times on a given weekend. Once a church adds a fourth worship service, only the rare pastor can continue to preach with energy at all services. Some medium churches have successfully developed multiple congregations by permanently assigning an associate pastor to preach at one or two additional worship services. While this takes at least two gifted communicators with high loyalty and trust in each other, it can be done. When successfully implemented, the church moves beyond multiple cell to multiple congregation.

Growth strategy 5 for medium churches is to *write a long-range plan*. Plans give a church direction and motivate members with a sense of purpose. The planning process does not have to be complicated but it should take into account the needs of the congregation, the opportunities to reach their target area for Christ, the resources available to fulfill the plan, and an outline of the steps to get started. Ask key questions like:

What business are we in today?

What dominates our thinking and our agenda?

What positions do our most dedicated people hold?

What is God calling us to do in the next five to ten years?

What difference would it make if we obeyed his call?

Medium churches need to avoid planning solely to remove problems or weaknesses. It is far better to develop a plan based on the congregation's strengths. Thus a key question is What do we do best?

Resist the temptation to think small. Medium churches are *not* small churches. Yet the people may persist in thinking of their church in small-size terms. When developing a long-range plan, a medium-sized church must think big. Thinking big allows the medium church to:

- innovate
- focus on opportunity
- embrace change
- take calculated risks
- dream God's dream for the future

Growth strategy 6 for medium churches is to *improve the quality of ministry.* It is not a secret that people today have higher expectations for their church than ever before. My mentor suggested that as a rule, a medium church's ministries and facilities need to be a notch above what its constituency expects or even needs. There are always exceptions, but most people lean toward attending a church that is slightly above their socioeconomic position in life. This means if people live, work, and play in air conditioning, they not only expect their church to be air conditioned, but they expect it to be a notch better than theirs at home. Parents do not want the child care at their church to be as good as what they use during the week—they want it a notch better. Those with super sound systems in their car and home will expect their church's sound system to be excellent. Thus it is vitally important to upgrade ministries as much as feasible to enhance the overall service level of the church.

There are five core areas that medium churches must focus on first: facilities, worship, children's ministries, leadership, and staff. A study conducted of those who do not attend church asked the question, "If you were to attend church, what would you look for?" The two main answers were a worship service that does not bore and excellent child care. Both of these two ministries must be housed in a facility that adds to their excellence. For these ministries to be upgraded, the church leadership and staff must grow along with the church. One of the most difficult realities to face in medium-sized churches is the fact that the leaders and staff who helped grow the church from small to medium may not be able to take it any farther. Improving the quality of the ministry means also improving the quality of pastoral and lay leaders. Ongoing leadership training is a must in the medium church if it is to continue growing beyond the medium size. While a medium church may have grown due to one or two effective ministries, it will plateau if it does not continually "notch up" the overall quality of its pastoral staff and leaders along with the facilities and ministry programs.

Different issues must be understood and faced at each stage of development. So Bob moved quickly along to discuss strategies for larger churches.

Growth strategy 1 for large churches is *renew the vision*. For a church to grow, it needs a vision. At one time, all large churches had a compelling vision. That is why they are where they are today. In the process of growing larger, however, they may have either fulfilled their original vision or stopped communicating it because they assume that everyone knows what it is. Both possibilities are danger signs for the large church.

Since vision is the key to long-term existence, a lost or forgotten vision places a large church in an atmosphere of aimless drifting. Eventually all of the congregation's energy and resources are spent maintaining the present. Growth slows into plateau, and plateau drops into decline. Disregarding vision ultimately causes the large church to lack the following:

- purpose
- direction
- motivation
- endeavor
- creativity

To continue growing as in the past, a large church must recast and communicate its vision regularly to the congregation. As the church grows larger and correspondingly more complex, it is necessary to have a simplified statement of vision set forth in a short phrase so the attenders can remember it.

Bob told of one larger church that formulated a forty-seven-word vision statement. They found that the people were unable to remember such a long statement or become passionate over it. The church leaders reviewed their vision in an attempt to arrive at a short statement the entire church could understand and own. After several meetings they eventually reduced their forty-seven-word statement to only ten words. Then they used the shortened statement to communicate the vision to the congregation. Because of Bob's experience in a large church, he highly recommends that the vision of this size church be communicated at least once a month from the pulpit, as well as in a minimum of five additional ways so that the entire congregation knows what the vision is.

Growth strategy 2 for large churches is to *design an assimilation plan.* The challenge of growth in larger churches can be compared to a profit and loss ledger. On the profit side of the ledger, larger churches usually do quite well. Their wide-open front door attracts newcomers in fairly large numbers. On the other side of the ledger, larger churches often do quite poorly. Their wide-open back door allows newcomers to drift away from the church rather than become involved in significant numbers. Thus one of the main hurdles to overcome in the larger church is balancing the "income-outgo" ledger.

The way to balance this ledger is by designing and implementing a routine assimilation process. Such a process generally involves all or most of the following.

1. A pastor is designated to be responsible for organizing, deploying, and maintaining the assimilation process.
2. A team or committee is put in place to work under the pastor of assimilation. This team carefully, systematically, and regularly monitors the assimilation of each newcomer. Tracking newcomers usually goes on for only one year due to the large number of new people constantly coming through the front door of the church. Ongoing assimilation occurs when the newcomer becomes involved in groups or classes during the first year.
3. A clearly defined and communicated process for becoming involved in the life of the church is established. This process includes at least some of the following: an orientation class or group that initiates newcomers into the values, purpose, and vision of the church; a way to involve newcomers into a group or class whereby they begin to receive regular care, love, and support; a way to recruit, train, and deploy newcomers into ministry inside and outside the church family.
4. The uniting of new people with the church is celebrated regularly.
5. A continuous evaluation of the effectiveness of the entire assimilation process is conducted and the process is adjusted to keep it up-to-date.

Growth strategy 3 for large churches is *streamline procedures.* To combat the tendency of the larger church toward bureaucracy, you must cut the fat! The fat is the sacred cows, the outdated, flabby systems and practices that have become standard operating procedure and "the way it's always been done." Another popular term for this is "decentralize."

Larger churches grow as they develop an organizational structure that allows them to take advantage of ministry opportunities in a reasonable amount of time, which means before the "hot" opportunity is "cold." Among other things this means using temporary task forces, rather than long-standing committees. The motto of the large church regarding operating procedures is:

If one person can get the job done, why use a committee?

According to my mentor, large churches streamline their structures by:

- defining their core values and living by them
- structuring systems to fulfill their purpose and vision
- minimizing differences in nonessential areas to maximize ministry potential
- empowering lay members to fulfill their own God-given dreams
- encouraging an atmosphere in which new ministry ideas can be attempted without fear.

Growth strategy 4 for large churches is *offer need-based events*. If you go to the average supermarket you will discover new products almost weekly. Labels say "diet," "sugar free," and "low fat." Why? Because manufacturers listen to the public's requests.

In the past, churches adopted programs that were designed at denominational headquarters and they expected people in the community to participate. Today's large church needs to totally reverse that approach by discovering people's needs and developing ministries to meet them.

This is important to the larger church for at least five reasons.

1. Need-based ministries become entry-level events where the unchurched may connect with the church's larger ministry.
2. Need-based ministries care for people in relevant ways right where they are in life.
3. Need-based ministries meet people when they are most open to receiving Christ as their Savior.
4. Need-based ministries keep the church from developing an inward looking mentality.
5. Need-based ministries carry on the Lord's own example of healing the sick and the lame and feeding the hungry.

Growth strategy 5 for large churches is *adjust leadership roles.* As a church grows, the leadership roles played by the pastor, staff, governing board, and supporting committees must change if the church is to continue its emergence as a large church. There are at least three key adjustments that must take place.

1. The congregational members must mature so that they allow their chosen leaders to lead. Small churches, of course, are often led by the congregation, with the pastor expected to carry out their sense of calling and priorities. As the small church grows through the medium size into a large church, a significant adjustment must take place. The congregation must become willing followers of their chosen leaders. Among the many adjustments needed in this process is the delegation of most of the decision making from the congregation to the leaders. From a practical viewpoint this usually means the congregation reserves the right to call the senior pastor, vote to indebt the

congregation, fire the senior pastor, change the constitution and doctrinal statement, and choose their lay leaders. All other decisions they leave in the hands of their chosen leaders.

2. The governing board must change from being a decision-making board to becoming a policy-setting board. In the medium church the governing board and standing committees most often make the decisions. However, as the church becomes larger, the members of these boards and committees normally do not maintain enough contact with the totality of the church's ministry to be able to make day-to-day, week-to-week, or month-to-month decisions. Since the paid staff is most knowledgeable about the church, it falls to the staff members to be the decision makers. The governing board and standing committees' main role becomes that of setting basic policy within which the paid staff make the decisions. To miss making this adjustment normally extends the decision-making process out to the point where the church begins to do a slow walk rather than a crisp run.

3. The senior pastor must exercise directive leadership. All the studies completed on growing churches in the last half century include one common denominator: The pastor accepts and exercises a strong leadership role. In smaller churches the pastor leads from a strong relational role. In medium churches the pastor leads from a strong administrative role. But in the large church the pastor must lead from a strong directive role. In part this means that the congregation expects the pastor to declare a sense of direction and the way to get there. No longer can the pastor afford to take a neutral position. The pastor must have a strong sense of purpose, vision, and hope for the church. He must accept the role of "leader among leaders," taking responsibility to influence the church by casting the vision for the church.

Growth strategy 6 for large churches is to *increase the number of small groups.* Effective larger churches emulate the qualities of small churches. Bob calls this the Less Is More Principle.

To get bigger you have to get smaller.

As churches grow larger and larger, their efficiencies steadily decrease, particularly in the area of member care. Once a certain economy of scale is reached, bigger is no longer better but can be worse.

My mentor suggested a good example from our world of business and commerce. Americans have always embraced the thinking of their pioneer forefathers looking to the horizons, pushing the borders of their frontiers, and striving to grow larger. The Japanese, on the other hand, confined by the physical size of their country, have found ways to become more productive by working with small units. The Japanese companies have continued to grow by getting progressively smaller.

Larger churches around the world have followed this same Less Is More Principle by emulating small churches. As they have grown larger, they have added more small groups within which people may receive the same level of care once thought only possible in the smaller church. From a practical perspective, larger churches need six to seven small groups for every hundred people over the age of thirteen in their congregation. Large churches that reach this number of small groups typically discover that between 50 and 60 percent of their adults attend one of the groups. However, to reach this level of small group involvement, it is almost always necessary to have a full-time pastor directing the process of development.

Bob had given me more ideas than I could possibly put into practice right away, but I was glad we had discussed ideas for all three sizes of church and not just those for my small church. At least now

I know what I will be facing as my church begins to grow. I trust my brief explanation of them will be as helpful to you as learning about them was for me and my church.

By the time Bob had finished explaining the different growth strategies for small, medium, and large churches, we had gone almost two hours longer than our normal time. We felt bad for our waitress who had to keep filling our coffee cups, and we left her an extra large tip. By then we both had to run to make other appointments.

Taking It Home

The growth strategies Bob suggested for the small church were the most significant to my current ministry, but you may be in a different situation. After looking over the strategies for all three sizes of church, which ones do you sense are most crucial for further developing your church? List the three most important ones below. Remember, churches that are in transition from one size to another may find strategies from any size church helpful.

Key Growth Strategies for My Church

Key Strategy 1:

Key Strategy 2:

Key Strategy 3:

12

Where To from Here?

AT THIS POINT, I SUPPOSE you are wondering what happened after Bob and I stopped meeting together. In short, a lot! It has been five years now since I made that first concerned call. When I look back and think how much has changed, I say a short prayer of thanks! As I applied the concepts I learned from Bob, my congregation and leaders became more responsive to my leadership. I will share some insights shortly about what I learned, but let me pause here to reflect on the process I used to turn my church around.

I did eventually attend the One Size Doesn't Fit All seminar. It was there I learned about a three-phase plan that I employed to turn my church around. The three phases are:

Add; Divide; Multiply!

In *Phase 1: Add*, I focused on adding a few new people to the church family. This phase prepared my congregation to accept new people. I began by praising the key members of my small church for the years of love and care they had bestowed on each other. Later I preached a sermon series that I titled "Caring for the Stranger." I used a passage from the Old Testament book of Leviticus 19:34 that has always intrigued me. It says, "The stranger who resides with you shall be to you as the native among you, and you shall love him as yourself; for you were aliens in the land of Egypt: I am the LORD your God." In that series of messages I stressed the concern of God for people outside the church family and that we are to love the strangers who come into our church. A few months later I returned to that same theme with a series built around the word *hospitality*, which means "love of strangers." Those two sermon series helped communicate the key values of love, care, concern, and openness to newcomers.

Shortly after becoming their pastor, I realized that my members knew a great deal *about* each other but they really did not *know* each other. Believing it was impossible for them to talk to newcomers until they learned to talk with each other, I organized a plan whereby all the members invited each other to their homes for dinner. This helped renew the skills of hospitality that they would need to welcome strangers in the coming year. During this same time, my wife and I, along with another couple in the church, worked hard at welcoming and assimilating guests into our church.

All of these efforts cracked the door open to newcomers. We added twenty-eight new members during the year, which proved to be a crucial step in preparing the church for future challenges. These initial changes successfully built an evangelism consciousness among the people and this provided the foundation for the next phase.

In *Phase 2: Divide*, we made the controversial move to two worship services. As my mentor had cautioned, this proved to be a difficult but necessary step toward becoming a multiple cell church. I spent almost an entire year meeting with my leaders and sharing with them the positive reasons why our church needed to divide into two worship services. Not surprisingly their main concern was the loss of fellowship, or rather the loss of seeing each other every week. I was able to overcome these objections by doing three things. First, I encouraged the board members to give two worship services a chance for a trial period of six months. I assured them that after the six-month test we would evaluate the services and decide at that time whether to continue with the two worship services or return to a single one. After the six-month trial period, the leaders decided to stay with two worship services. Second, I established a fellowship time between the two services. Our first worship service ran from 9:00 A.M. to 10:15 A.M. We followed that with an all-church fellowship time from 10:15 to 10:45. Then the second worship service ran from 11:00 A.M. to 12:15 P.M. This all-church fellowship time allowed the members to see each other, even though they attended different services. We offered two Sunday school sessions concurrently with the two worship services. Third, I met privately with several of the long-term members and asked them to attend different services. Enough of them agreed to do so that it effectively separated the original single cell into two separate cells.

We are still in *Phase 3: Multiplication.* Once the move to two worship services was accepted, I continued to multiply new units by adding several classes and groups. For example, the women's mission group had been declining for a number of years. Younger women who attended the missions group did not feel it was meeting their needs. My wife and I hosted a meeting with five of the younger women and encouraged them to begin a new group. They accepted the challenge, and we now have two women's groups. Women who are new to our church seem to find a more open spirit in the new group.

I also encouraged the men to add two new basketball teams to the church's sports ministry. Only one church basketball team had entered the city league in past years. It had provided good fellowship for the men in the church but not much outreach into the community. Now we have three teams, and players are encouraged to invite their unchurched friends to play. In the first year of this arrangement, three men accepted Christ as their Savior and six new families joined the church through this ministry. My plan is to keep multiplying new ministries as we continue to become a multi-cell church.

The average worship attendance in our church is now close to 280 on Sunday mornings. I know we are facing new challenges, but with what I have learned about different size churches, I now have a handle on how to move ahead. As you can imagine, I have had several "aha" experiences, which may be of interest to you.

First, I discovered that some people say they want the church to grow, but what they really mean is they do not want the church to die. Early in my ministry I assumed every church wanted to grow. I soon learned, however, that what members really want is growth that makes no demands to change. Starting and stopping something requires much greater energy than just letting it be. Many churches practice two general rules: (1) If it is moving, don't try to stop it. (2) If it is still, don't try to move it. This concept applies to more than physical objects. It is difficult to break an old habit or form a new one. Traditions resist change, and new ideas seldom gain an immediate following. What this means is a leader needs to look for "rocks under the wheels." Growing a church is like a car going downhill. Once it is started and has momentum, it can run over bumps. But a rock stuck under a wheel can prevent a stopped car from rolling. Fewer than 10 percent of active members can keep a church from moving, particularly the small church. It is crucial to find and remove these "rocks," or what my mentor called obstacles, before the church will invest enough energy to start moving.

Second, I learned that the main reason churches get into trouble is because leaders have taken their eyes off what the church is all about. Many of our congregations need to go back and rethink what they have been commissioned by God to do. This involves writing a fresh purpose statement based on the timeless principles of God's Word. Church leaders must always keep their eyes on what the church is about and work on keeping their church on track. "Small, medium, or large churches all succeed the same way: by knowing what business they are in," my mentor used to say. I believe it is important for all churches to answer three key questions regardless of their size:

1. What was our church's original dream?
2. Has that dream changed or been reached?
3. If so, what is God's dream for us today?

Until we ask and answer those questions, we will continue in crisis.

Third, I discovered that church leaders usually see problems but they do not realize how severe the problems are. The leaders of my church knew that guests were coming and going but they felt the problem would simply work itself out. After a while they just became used to the problem, "like a couple of pounds you've added to your waistline." As a pastor, I found it was part of my responsibility to assist my leaders in discovering whether the problems we faced were temporary or permanent. Were they long-term illnesses or short-term aches that would gradually go away? Each time our board met, I would ask questions like, "What exactly is the issue? Will it go away by itself? If not, What opportunities does it present to us?"

Fourth, I discovered that growing churches are full of paradoxes. Four particular ones come to mind. One paradox is: Growing churches *win some, lose some.* While new people have joined my church, others have left. Some people are attracted to one particular size church. As a church grows, they may no longer feel they fit into the new size church and eventually leave for a church more the size they like. It pains me to see anyone leave, but it is going to happen.

I call the second paradox *tune in, tune out.* It is wise to learn when to listen to people and act, as well as when to listen to people and not act. Each complaint demands a listening ear. When a lady anguished over her marriage, I listened. When a family member was in the hospital, I listened. When someone told me of an unsaved friend, I listened. However, when people complained that the sanctuary was too cold, I did little. A leader cannot please everyone.

The third paradox is *tear down, build up*. To make room for new people, we regularly faced decisions about remodeling and building new facilities. We tore out an old parking lot and repaved it to accommodate more cars. We also dismantled a nonfunctional budget and retooled the church's finances to meet ministry needs.

The fourth paradox is *good days, bad days*. Rarely does anyone hear about the valley of the shadow of church growth, but it exists. I recall some bad days when attendance sagged, finances plummeted, and spirits drooped due to layoffs caused by economic conditions in our church community. We stayed focused on our long-range plans, however, and anticipated the good. Good days eventually came when people accepted Christ, attendance exceeded predictions, and new ministries took root. Both good and bad days are faced in the pursuit of a great dream.[22]

Fifth, I discovered that any size church must have in place what I call Home Base Ministries before it can add a lot of newer creative ministries. People expect churches to have a certain ministry base regardless of the church size. The six Home Base Ministries that I believe churches need are children's ministry, youth ministry, Christian education, worship, administration, and finance. Over the past three years we have worked hard to get these key ministries in place. Now that they are up and going, we can focus on adding cutting-edge programs to expand our church.

Sixth, I discovered that it is wise to give people a wide latitude in developing new ministry ideas. My board now sees its calling as empowering members' ideas for ministry rather than vetoing them. All we ask is that ministry teams remain compatible with our doctrine, morals, ethics, money, and staff. If members have a creative idea for a new ministry, we ask them to find five additional people in the church to work with them, to develop a plan showing how the new ministry will fulfill our church's mission statement, and then to present the plan to the governing board. To date we have seen three new ministries started but we hope for many more in the next year.

The greatest lesson I have learned is that it is important to have a plan for the future. The final question to be faced is always, Where to from here? The old saying is true, "If you fail to plan, you plan to fail." Thus I highly recommend that you do the following.

- **Keep praying.** Prayer is a powerful ingredient for developing a climate for growth. Challenge your people to pray for the community. Assign people to pray for each block or square mile or subdivision. List unchurched friends, neighbors, family members, and others within your ministry area. Ask your people to pray for people on their lists regularly by name and for their salvation.
- **Face the facts.** It is wise to ask a lot of questions to help you discover the truth about your church's current situation. The following questions are often key: What size is our church? What opportunities does our size church have for future growth? What has God accomplished through our church in the past? What opportunities has he given us for the future? What growth obstacles are in the way of achieving God's dream for our church? How can such obstacles be turned into opportunities?
- **Communicate your vision.** Your church must have a compelling vision from God that lends itself to direction. As the church begins to grow larger, frustrations develop without continuous communication of the vision. Bob told me that "as a general rule, people in a church forget the vision in about two weeks and staff forget it in about four weeks." You will get tired of sharing your vision before your people get it.
- **Expose your leaders to** *One Size Doesn't Fit All.* As your church grows, take the time to assist your leaders to understand the kinds of changes that will need to take place. A good way to do that is to study my story in this book. You will see lights turn on in people's minds as they begin to understand that you are not just getting larger but are becoming different as well.

- **Maintain care.** One of the first problems in the early church arose when they were "increasing in number." A "complaint arose . . . because their widows were being overlooked" (Acts 6:1). The first problem experienced by the early church was the issue of member care! As new people come into a church, there must be ways to care for them. Systems of care should be provided for both long-term members and newer ones so no one senses he or she is lost in a crowd.
- **Wait patiently.** You cannot lead your church to grow if you cannot take the time to plow, plant, water, and weed before you harvest. The harvest cannot be rushed. Set goals that can be reached and celebrated while you wait and work. The great soccer player Pele once said,

Success is not how many games you win, but how hard you practice after you lose.

That is a good motto for us to follow in the church. Many times our efforts will not produce the results we expect. We must not give up but keep working with God to create the climate for growth.

The opportunity I had to share my frustrations and learn from my mentor turned my life, and my church, around. I am reminded of the benefits of understanding the different size churches every day. As I sit in my office, obstacles and opportunities still confront the church I serve. However, by understanding the principle of *One Size Doesn't Fit All*, I have a good idea of what is coming next and the steps my church needs to take to get to the next size church.

The last time I had breakfast with Bob, he challenged me to begin mentoring someone else in the principles of *One Size Doesn't Fit All*. Thus besides all the changes in my own ministry, I am now going to share my insights with others.

Why don't you give me a call and let's talk?

Notes

Chapter 1 What Size Are You?

1. A study conducted by the Church Growth Institute of Lynchburg, Virginia, surveyed 1,000 churches of various sizes. Of 464 responses, 54 percent stated that the same problems exist in smaller and larger churches. See the article "Myth #3: Smaller Churches Have Different Problems than Larger Churches" (Lynchburg, Va.: Church Growth Institute, n.d.).

2. For further information on Church Size Strategies, write Dr. Bill M. Sullivan, Church of the Nazarene, Division of Church Growth, 6401 The Paseo, Kansas City, MO 64131.

3. Adapted from Lyle E. Schaller, "Looking at Churches by Type," *Church Management* (April 1972), 7.

Chapter 2 What Is the Church's Orientation?

4. Quoted by C. Wayne Zunkel in *Growing the Small Church: A Guide for Church Leaders* (Elgin, Ill.: David C. Cook, 1984), 3.

5. Jim Kerr, "Hey, Small Church! Lift Your Head High!" *Growing Churches* (April, May, June, 1991), 3.

6. Lyle E. Schaller, "Music in the Large Church," *Choristers Guild Letters* 21, no. 7 (March 1980): 28.

7. Adapted from Carl Dudley, "Fundamentally Different Orientations in Life," *The Five Stones* (summer 1993), 7–8.

8. Schaller's research was gathered from a database of 125,000 churches and 20 denominations. For the full report, see Lyle E. Schaller, "What Is Your Favorite Number?" *Net Results* (May 1997), 13–14.

9. Lyle E. Schaller, "Are Midsize Churches an Endangered Species?" *Net Results* (August 1996), 5.

Chapter 4 Who Sets the Direction?

10. Quote in C. B. Hogue, "Spiritual Leadership," *Growing Churches* (winter 1995), 10.

11. Quoted in Lovett Weems Jr., *Church Leadership* (Nashville: Abingdon Press), 19–20.

Chapter 5 What Is the Pastor's Role?

12. Portions of this chapter are adapted from Lyle E. Schaller, "What Does Your Pastor Do Best?" *The Christian Ministry* 15, no. 2 (March 1984): 27–28.

13. John C. Maxwell, *Developing the Leader within You* (Nashville: Thomas Nelson, 1993), 1–17.

Chapter 6 How Are Decisions Made?

14. Adapted from John D. Huff, "Five Guiding Principles of Effective Church Ministry," *Effective Decision-Making for Church Leaders* (Monrovia, Calif.: Church Growth, Inc., 1988), 2–5.

Chapter 7 What Is the Impact of Staff?

15. John Vaughan, "What It Takes to Be a Growth Leader," *Growing Churches* (October, November, December, 1993), 55.

16. L. Ronald Brushwyler, "Bi-Vocational Pastors: A Research Report," *The Five Stones* (spring 1994), 8.

17. Reported by Dale E. Jones, "Research and Trends," *GROW* 4, no. 1 (spring 1993), 57.

Chapter 9 How Do Churches Grow?

18. Charles Van Engen refers to this desire as a "yearning" for church growth. See Charles Van Engen, *The Growth of the True Church* (Amsterdam: Rodopi, 1977).

19. Dale E. Jones, "Research and Trends," *GROW* (summer 1994), 53.

20. Dale E. Jones, "Research and Trends," *GROW* (spring 1998), 55.

21. Adapted from Nicholas B. van Dyck, "Get Ready, Get Set, Invite a Friend," *Net Results* (June 1990), 3–7.

Chapter 12 Where To from Here?

22. Adapted from John Duncan, "Church-Growth Paradoxes," *Growing Churches* (October, November, December, 1993), 7–8.

Dr. Gary L. McIntosh is a nationally known author, speaker, educator, consultant, and professor of Christian Ministry and Leadership at Talbot School of Theology, Biola University, located in La Mirada, California. He has written extensively in the field of pastoral ministry, leadership, generational studies, and church growth.

Dr. McIntosh received his B.A. from Colorado Christian University in Biblical Studies, an M.Div. from Western C.B. Seminary in Pastoral Studies, and a D.Min. from Fuller Theological Seminary in Church Growth Studies.

As president of The McIntosh Church Growth Network, a church-consulting firm he founded in 1989, Dr. McIntosh has served more than 500 churches in 53 denominations throughout the United States and Canada. The 1995 and 1996 president of the American Society for Church Growth, he edits both the *Church Growth Network* newsletter and the *Journal of the American Society for Church Growth*.

Dr. Gary L. McIntosh speaks to numerous churches, organizations, schools, and conventions each year. Services available include keynote presentations at major meetings, seminars and workshops, training courses, and ongoing consultation.

For a live presentation of the material found in *One Size Doesn't Fit All* or to request a catalog of materials or other information on Dr. McIntosh's availability and ministry, contact:

The McIntosh Church Growth Network
P.O. Box 892589
Temecula, CA 92589-2589
909-506-3086
www.mcintoshcgn.com
www.churchgrowthnetwork.com